THE PROCESS OF
CULTURAL COMPETENCE
IN THE DELIVERY OF
HEALTHCARE SERVICES
A CULTURALLY COMPETENT MODEL OF CARE

JOSEPHA CAMPINHA-BACOTE

Acknowledgements and Dedication

Many people had a role in the publication of this book and I would like to personally acknowledge and thank them. I thank my family for their patience during the concentrated and intense periods of work on this edition. Specifically, I thank my husband for his unconditional support and motivation that inspired me to begin work on this edition. He also provided me with thoughtful revisions which I feel has added to the quality of this book. I also appreciate his taking our 9 year old daughter on "special outings" so I could have uninterrupted time to develop my manuscript. I thank my two teenage sons, ages 18 & 19, for timely interruptions that kept me focused on the important things -- them. I thank my 9 year old daughter for her feminine touch of helping me pick out the colors of this book cover as well as providing me with much hugs and kisses during the writing of this book. I also thank her for her encouraging comments; "Are you still working on that book; when will you be finished?"

I would like to acknowledge my parents, who provided me with a strong cultural background rooted in the Cape Verdean culture. I thank my mother for always being there throughout my educational process. She was there for the good times and the bad times. She always had a positive and encouraging word to say. It has been two years since my father died, and it is with sadness that I acknowledge that he is no longer in my immediate presence. However, I do feel his presence and thank him for always believing in me and being proud of my work. It is for him that I keep the "Campinha" as part of my formal last name.

I would like to thank my colleagues, from diverse cultural and ethnic backgrounds, who provided me with enriched opportunities to engage in cross-cultural encounters. This invaluable opportunity is hopefully reflected in this current edition of my book. I also thank my students who questioned my earlier models of cultural competence and provided me with insight to develop my current model.

I acknowledge and thank the above individuals as having an active part in the publication of this book, however, I dedicate this book to God. It is only through His blessings and His grace that I have acquired the desire, talent, commitment and knowledge to humbly contribute to the field of transcultural health care. I owe all my victories, successes, accomplishments and achievements to Him. All the glory and praise be to God!

Contents

Cultural Competence: Still a Vexing Problem

"You must be the change you wish in the world..."

Mahatma Gandhi

The concept of culture and its relationship to healthcare beliefs and practices is essential to comprehend when discussing cultural competence in healthcare delivery. Cultural values give an individual a sense of direction as well as meaning to life. These values are held on an unconscious level. As eloquently stated by Leininger (1967), "culture is tightly interwoven into the life of man and continuously pervades his thinking, actions, feelings and particularly his health state" (p. 37). The literature is saturated with definitions of culture. For the purpose of this book, Tylor's (1871) definition of culture will be used. Tylor defined culture as "that complex and whole which includes knowledge, belief, art, morals, law, custom and any other capabilities and habits acquired by man as a member of society" (p.1). As reflected by this definition, culture is not limited to racial classification and national origin. There are many other faces of cultural diversity. Religious affiliation, language, physical size, gender, sexual orientation, age, disability (both physical and mental), political orientation, socio-economic status, occupational status and geographical location are but a few of the faces of cultural diversity (Campinha-Bacote, 2003).

The changing demographics and economics of our growing multicultural world and the long-standing disparities in the health status of people from culturally diverse backgrounds has challenged healthcare professionals and organizations to consider cultural diversity as a priority. In the 1960's, healthcare theorists from various disciplines began to develop theoretical and conceptual frameworks for assessing, planning and implementing culturally relevant services for culturally diverse populations (Purnell, 1998). A current review of the literature reveals that Cross, Bazron, Dennis & Isaac's (1989) definition of cultural competence has been the most widely accepted and utilized definition. These authors define cultural competence as "a set of congruent behaviors, attitudes, and policies that come together in a system, agency, or amongst professionals and enables that system, agency, or those professionals to work effectively in cross-cultural situations" (iv).

In 2000, the United States Department of Health and Human Services (USDHHS) Office of Minority Health released national standards for the provision of culturally and linguistically appropriate services (CLAS). CLAS is intended to be used as a means to address and correct inequities that exist in providing health care to culturally and ethnically diverse groups (Appendix A). In addition to the CLAS standards, there are currently many other resources available to healthcare professionals that address the issue of cultural competency and the provision of culturally and linguistically appropriate services (Appendix B). The purpose of this book is to present a model of cultural competence for healthcare professionals to enhance their journey towards cultural competence.

Chapter 1 presents background development of the model as well as revisions the model has undergone since 1991, including an overview of the current model of cultural competence, *The Process of Cultural Competence in the Delivery of Healthcare Services.* Chapters 2 through 6 define and discuss each construct of this model. Chapter 7 briefly discusses applications of the model and concludes by giving healthcare professionals one example of the clinical application of the model. Appendices A through C provide healthcare professionals with resources for further enhancing their journey towards cultural competence, while Appendix D presents a self-assessment tool (Inventory For Assessing the Process of Cultural Competence Among Healthcare Professionals - Revised [IAPCC-R]) for healthcare professionals. This tool is based on the model of cultural competence which is presented in this book. *Now, let the journey begin!*

CHAPTER 1

Development Of The Model

"We are never more alive than when it hurts..."

Fredrick Buechner

The developmental stages of my current model of cultural competence, *The Process of Cultural Competence in the Delivery of Healthcare Services*, dates back to 1969, when I was pursuing an undergraduate degree in Connecticut. During this time period there was a great unrest and conflict in the area of race relations. It was very clear that one had to identify as being either Black or White. Being a second generation Cape Verdean and raised in an exclusively Cape Verdean community, I found myself not fitting into either racial group. This experience brought about the painful process of coming to terms with my self-identification and cultural heritage. However, it also brought me to a place of passion and interest in the area of culturally and ethnically diverse groups. This is where my journey began.

I completed my baccalaureate, masters and doctoral degrees in nursing and extended my interest in diverse cultural groups to the fields of transcultural nursing and medical anthropology. In addition, my clinical background as a psychiatric nurse led me to explore the fields of multicultural counseling and transcultural psychiatry. In 2002, I entered the seminary to begin pursuit of a graduate degree in theological studies. It is a blending of these fields of study that led to the development of my model of cultural competence in healthcare delivery. *The Process of Cultural Competence in the Delivery of Healthcare Services* model blends the works of Madeleine Leininger (1978) in the area of transcultural nursing, Paul

Development of the Model

Pedersen (1988) in the area of multicultural counseling, Arthur Klienman (1978) in the area of transcultural psychiatry, and Eric Law (1993) in the areas of theology and multicultural ministry.

In 1991, I developed the first version of my model called, *The Process of Cultural Competence: A Culturally Competent Model of Care* (figure 1). In this original model, I identified four constructs of cultural competence: cultural awareness, cultural knowledge, cultural skill, and cultural encounters. The pictorial representation of this model led one to believe that the process of cultural competence was linear. This led me to revise the pictorial representation of my model.

In 1998, I revised my model to include a fifth construct of cultural competence -- cultural desire. In addition, I redefined the construct of cultural knowledge to include the emerging fields of genetics, ethnic pharmacology and other current issues in biocultural ecology. I also revised the pictorial representation of the model. In contrast to my earlier model that pictorially reflected a linear process of cultural competence, the revised model depicted five interlocking circles. These interlocking circles revealed the true dynamic and interdependent relationship between the five constructs (figure 2).

From 1998 to 2002, I further developed the construct of cultural desire, which resulted in the final pictorial revision of my model. This evolved model depicts the process of cultural competence as a volcano. The volcano symbolically represents that it is cultural desire which evokes the process of cultural competence. When the volcano erupts (desire), it brings forth the desire to enter into the process of becoming culturally competent by seeking cultural encounters, obtaining cultural knowledge, conducting culturally-sensitive assessments and being humble to the process of cultural awareness (figure 3).

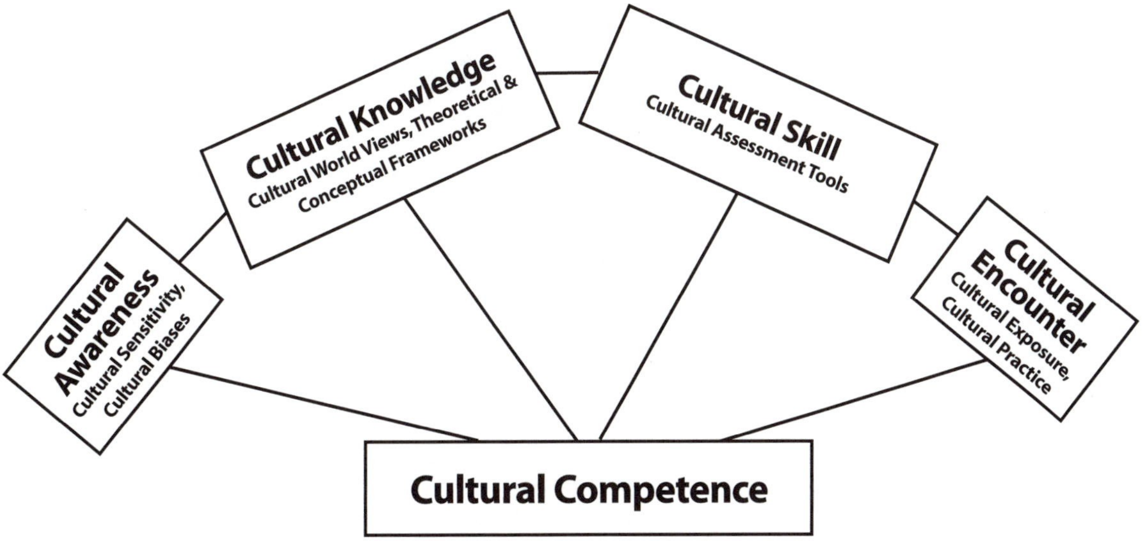

A Culturally Competent Model of Care

(Campinha-Bacote, 1991)

Figure 1

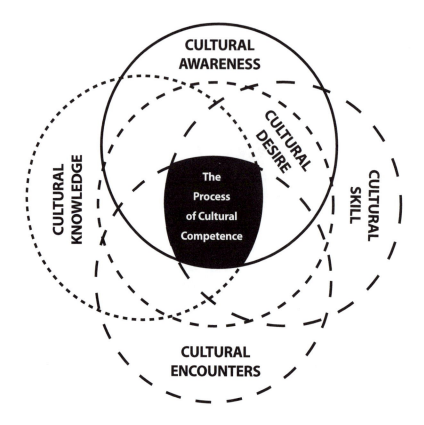

The Process of Cultural Competence in the Delivery of Healthcare Services

(Campinha-Bacote, 1998)

Figure 2

The Process of Cultural Competence in the Delivery of Healthcare Services

(Campinha-Bacote, 2002)

Figure 3

Development Of The Model

The Process of Cultural Competence in the Delivery of Healthcare Services is a model that views cultural competence as the ongoing process in which the healthcare professional continuously strives to achieve the ability and availability to work effectively within the cultural context of the client (individual, family, community). This model requires healthcare professionals to see themselves as *becoming* culturally competent rather than *being* culturally competent. The process involves the integration of cultural desire, cultural awareness, cultural knowledge, cultural skill and cultural encounters. The assumptions of the model are:

1. Cultural competence is a process; not an event.
2. The process of cultural competence consists of five inter-related constructs: cultural desire, cultural awareness, cultural knowledge, cultural skill and cultural encounters.
3. The key and pivotal construct of cultural competence is cultural desire.
4. There is more variation within cultural groups than across cultural groups (intra-cultural variation).
5. There is a direct relationship between a healthcare professionals' level of cultural competence and their ability to provide culturally responsive healthcare services.
6. Cultural competence is an essential component in rendering effective and culturally responsive care to all clients.

CHAPTER 2

Cultural Desire

"The starting point of all achievement is desire.
Weak desires bring weak results..."

Napoleon Hill

Cultural desire is defined as the motivation of the healthcare professional to "want to" engage in the process of becoming culturally competent; not the "have to" (Campinha-Bacote, 1998). This motivation is genuine and authentic, with no hidden agendas. Rogers (1951) states that genuineness, or congruence, is the very basic ability of a person to read his own inner experiencing and allow the quality of this inner experiencing to be apparent in the relationship. The concepts of caring and platonic love are central to the construct of cultural desire.

Rollo May describes care as "a state in which something does matter; it is the source of human tenderness." It has been said that people don't care how much you know, until they first know how much you care. This type of caring "comes from the heart; not from the mouth" (Campinha-Bacote, 1998). The goal is not to offer comments that are politically correct (words from the mouth), but rather to offer comments to the client that reflect true caring (words from the heart).

It is my belief that the reason which motivates one to want to engage in the process of cultural competence is based on the humanistic value of caring and loving one another. We are all unique individuals who belong to the same race - the human race, with similar basic human needs. Our goal in providing culturally responsive care is to find common ground. As stated by Bernard Baruch, "We did not all come over on the same ship, but we are all in the same boat." In the Bible, the Book of Romans has the following verses that healthcare professionals may want to reflect on for grasping the concepts of caring and platonic love:

"Be kindly affectioned one to another with brotherly love; in honor preferring one another"
Romans 12:10

"Owe no man any thing, but to love one another: for he that loveth hath fulfilled the law"
Romans 13:8

Cultural desire also involves a commitment of personal sacrifice. One must be willing to sacrifice one's prejudice and biases towards culturally different clients in order to develop cultural desire. This sacrifice also involves the moral commitment to care for all clients, regardless of their cultural values, beliefs or practices. However, this task may be difficult when caring for challenging clients who engage in behaviors that may be in direct moral conflict with the healthcare professional (e.g., abortion, spouse abuse, sexual addictions). For example, how does a healthcare professional care for an Arab client whose political and/or religious beliefs are in direct contrast to their beliefs? As healthcare professionals we do not have to like the client's behavior, however, we must treat the person as a unique human being worthy and deserving of our love and care. Cultural desire comes from one's aspiration, and not out of one's desperation. "We must never look down upon someone unless we are helping them up" (Reverend Jesse Jackson).

Cultural desire includes a genuine passion and commitment to be open and flexible with others; a respect for differences, yet a commitment to build upon similarities; a willingness to learn from clients and others as cultural informants; and a sense of humility. However, there is a paradox in possessing humility, for when we become aware of our humility, we've lost

Cultural Desire

it. Therefore, humility can be viewed as a by-product of cultural desire and not a sought after character trait to be mastered.

It is desire that creates our future (Allender, 1999). If healthcare professionals want to create a future of rendering culturally responsive services, it will have to be driven by desire. Desire is the fuel necessary to draw one into their personal journey towards cultural competence.

CHAPTER 3

Cultural Awareness

"The life which is not examined,
is the life not worth living..."

Socrates

Cultural awareness is the self-examination and in-depth exploration of one's own cultural background (Campinha-Bacote, 1998). This process involves the recognition of one's biases, prejudices and assumptions about individuals who are different. Without being aware of the influence of one's own cultural values, there is risk that the healthcare professional may engage in cultural imposition. Cultural imposition is the tendency to impose one's beliefs, values and patterns of behavior upon another culture (Leininger, 1978). Lara (1997) suggests the following self-examination and self-awareness questions that healthcare professionals may consider when answering the question, "Where are you in your journey toward cultural awareness?"

1. What cultural/ethnic group, socio-economic class, religion, age, and community do you belong to?
2. What experiences have you had with people from cultural groups, socio-economic classes, religions, age groups, or communities different from yourself?
3. How did you feel about them?
4. When you were growing up, what did your parents and significant others say about people who were different from your family?
5. What about your cultural/ethnic group, religion, socio-economic class, age or community did you feel embarrassing or wish you could change?
6. What personal qualities do you have that will help you establish interpersonal relations with persons from other cultures?
7. What personal qualities may be detrimental?

Cultural Awareness

In seeking cultural awareness there must be a commitment to cultural openness and cultural humility. Cultural openness refers to a "lifelong stance that promotes cultural self awareness and continuing development of transcultural skills" (Wenger, 1998, p. 64). Wenger further adds that cultural openness connotes both cognition and emotion, whereby the human will is engaged in learning about transcultural similarities and differences. Similar to the concept of cultural openness, is cultural humility. Tervalon and Murray-Garcia (1998) define cultural humility as a life-long commitment to self-evaluation and self-critique, re-addressing the power imbalances in the client-healthcare professional relationship and developing mutual beneficial partnerships with communities on behalf of individuals and defined populations.

To better understand the dynamics of cultural awareness, it may be useful to imagine cultural awareness along a continuum that ranges from unconscious incompetence to unconscious competence (Campinha-Bacote, 1996; Purnell, 1998). There are four levels of cultural competence: unconscious competence, conscious incompetence, conscious competence and unconscious competence. These four stages are directly related to one's level of cultural awareness, or consciousness, regarding interactions with individuals outside one's cultural group.

Unconscious incompetence is being unaware that one is lacking cultural knowledge. This healthcare professional is not aware that cultural differences exist between themselves and the client. One expert describes this as the "cultural blind spot syndrome" (Buchwald et. al, 1994). Specifically, the healthcare professional may assume that there are no cultural differences because a particular client may look and behave much the same way the healthcare professional does. One example of the cultural blind spot syndrome is when the healthcare professional may believe that because a client is of the same ethnic group, they share similar values, beliefs, lifestyles and practices. This may be a faulty assumption based on the concept of intra-cultural variation. Intra-cultural variation means that there is more variation within cultural groups than across cultural groups.

Conscious incompetence is being aware that one is lacking knowledge about another cultural group (Purnell, 1998). Here, the healthcare professional is keenly aware that cultural differences exist. The healthcare professional may have realized this by attending a workshop on cultural diversity, reading an article or book on the topic, discussing cultural issues with peers, or having a direct cross-cultural experience with a client from a different cultural background. These healthcare professionals possess the "know that" knowledge, but not the "know how" knowledge. They know that culture plays a key role when interacting with others, but they do not know how to effectively communicate with clients from different cultural backgrounds.

Conscious competence is described by Purnell (1998) as the conscious act of learning about the client's culture, verifying generalizations and providing culturally relevant interventions. The consciously competent healthcare professional has personally experienced cross-cultural interactions and is extremely aware that cultural differences must be respected and understood in order to have successful and effective cross-cultural interactions. These healthcare professionals are deliberate in applying the cultural knowledge and principles they have learned, however, because of their limited encounters with clients from different cultural groups, these healthcare professionals may not feel comfortable when interacting with culturally diverse clients. One possible reason for this discomfort is the fear of not being "politically correct." Healthcare professionals at this level are overly conscious of doing and saying the right thing. At times, their political correctness can actually interfere with effective communication.

Unconscious competence is the ability of the healthcare professional to spontaneously provide culturally responsive care to clients from a diverse culture. These healthcare professionals have experienced many encounters with culturally diverse clients and have developed an intuitive grasp of how to easily and effectively communicate in cross-cultural encounters. The timing of unconsciously competent healthcare professionals is always accurate and they appear to be "a natural" when observed interacting with clients from culturally diverse backgrounds. However, Purnell (1998) states that "unconscious incompetence is difficult to accomplish ... most healthcare providers can expect to reach only the conscious competence stage of cultural development" (p. 2).

Anthropologist Milton Bennett suggests another view of cultural awareness that occurs along a continuum (adapted by Culhane-Pera, 1996). The healthcare professional begins at the position of avoidance and progresses to the final stage of integration. The first three stages along this continuum (avoidance, protection, and minimization) can be classified as ethnocentric stages. In the avoidance phase, the healthcare professional is totally unaware that others don't share the same worldview. In the protection stage healthcare professionals experience cultural differences as threatening to their own identity and views of reality. Healthcare professionals also attempt to minimize cultural differences while emphasizing the unifying aspects of humanity. The other end of the cultural awareness continuum reflects an ethnorelative perspective in which the healthcare professional accepts, adapts and integrates cultural differences into their practice. The healthcare professional realizes that Western medicine is limited and begins to respect and accept culturally different worldviews. At the final stage of cultural awareness, the healthcare professional realizes that the integration of different worldviews and approaches to healthcare are essential in caring for all clients.

Borkan and Neher's (1991) Development Model of Ethnosensitivity is still another framework that can assist healthcare professionals in becoming more appreciative of the values and behaviors within the context of special cultural norms. This developmental model assesses the healthcare professional's ability to grasp cross-cultural issues as well as suggests strategies for improving cross-cultural communication and practice skills. The authors also assert that ethnosensitivity can be viewed on a continuum of personal growth, advancing from ethnocentrism to ethnorelativity. This developmental model begins with the ethnocentric position of fear (mistrust) and progresses through the phases of denial (cultural blindness, over-generalization), superiority (negative stereotyping), minimization (reductionism), relativism (acceptance), empathy (pluralism) and finally, an ethnosensitive attitude of integration. It is important to understand that the level of sensitivity a healthcare professional exhibits is likely to vary according to the cultural group encountered. For example, a healthcare professional who has had more encounters with Southeast Asians than Native Americans may be ethnosensitive towards Southeast Asians and ethnocentric when interacting with Native Americans. Therefore, the developmental stages of ethnosensitivity should not be considered mutually exclusive (Borkan and Neher, 1991). The ultimate goals of Borkan and Neher's Developmental Model of Ethno-sensitivity are "fostering ethnosensitivity - the ability to appreciate values and behaviors within the context of specific cultural norms - and ethnosensitive praxis - the application of this ability to clinical practice" (p. 212).

   In progressing through the stages of cultural awareness, there are different interaction styles that the healthcare professional may consciously or unconsciously operate in. Bell & Evans (1981) describe five basic interpersonal styles that one may engage in when interacting with a client from another culture. *Overt racism* is when the healthcare professional interacts out of deep-seated prejudices that he/she has toward a particular cultural group. The healthcare professional will use the power of his/her attitudes and behaviors to dehumanize the client. *Covert racism* is an interacting style in which the healthcare professional is aware of his/her fears of a specific cultural group, but knows that open expression of those attitudes is inappropriate. The healthcare professional attempts to hide or "cover-up" his/her true feelings. *Cultural ignorance* is when the healthcare professional has little or no prior exposure to the specific cultural group and experiences fear due to his/her inability to relate to the client. The *color blind* healthcare professional denies the reality of cultural differences that are important for effective interactions. In this interacting style, the healthcare professional has made a decision that he/she is committed to equality for all people and therefore treats all people alike, regardless of cultural background. Finally, the *culturally-liberated* healthcare professional does not fear cultural differences and is aware of his/her attitude towards specific cultural groups. This healthcare professional encourages the client to express feelings about their ethnicity and uses these feelings as a shared learning experience. Healthcare professionals must be aware of what interacting style they are operating in and strive toward a culturally-liberated interacting style.

Bell & Evans (1981) openly discuss the issue of racism when describing styles of interaction. However, discussions on racism in health care are commonly avoided. Barbee (2002) adds that when the subject is racism, there is dialectical tension. Racism can be defined as "a situation in which one race maintains supremacy over another race through a set of attitudes, behaviors, social structures and ideologies" (Barbee, p. 194). The Women's Theological Center (cited in Barbee, 2002), maintains that racism, "involves four essential and interconnected elements: (a) Power: the disproportionately distributed capacity to make and enforce decisions; (b) Resources: unequal access to such resources such as money, education, information, etc.; (c) Standards: standards for appropriate behavior are ethnocentric, reflecting and privileging the norms and values of the dominant race/society; and (d) Problem: involves defining 'reality' by naming "the problem' incorrectly, and thus misplacing it" (p. 194).

In examining the construct of cultural awareness, healthcare professionals must examine racism and ask the question, "Is there racism in health care?" The American Nurses Association's Position Statement on Discrimination and Racism in Health Care (2002), states that, "Discrimination and racism continue to be a part of the fabric and tradition of American society and have adversely affected minority populations, the health care system in general, and the profession of nursing." In addition, a recent congressionally mandated report from the Institute of Medicine (IOM) reveals that a large body of research supports the findings that racial and ethnic minorities in the United States receive lower quality health care than Whites, even when insurance status, income, age and severity of condition are comparable (Smedley, Stith and Nelson, 2002). Examples of health care disparities found in the IOM Report note that minorities:

- are less likely to be given appropriate cardiac medications or to undergo bypass surgery;
- are less likely to receive kidney dialysis or transplants;
- are less likely to receive appropriate cancer diagnostic tests and treatments;
- are less likely to receive the most sophisticated treatments for HIV infections; and
- are more likely to receive some less desirable procedures, such as lower limb amputations for diabetes and other conditions.

Although a myriad of sources may contribute to the above disparities, evidence now suggests that racism on the part of the healthcare professional may also contribute to differences in care.

In discussing the topic of racism, McIntosh (1988) describes a phenomenon she calls white privilege. She states, "as a white person I was taught to see racism only in individual acts of meanness, not in invisible systems conferring dominance on my group." McIntosh acknowledges that being white (white privilege) allows her an invisible package of unearned assets that she can count on cashing in each day. Some examples she gives of white privilege are:

- I can go shopping alone most of the time, pretty well assured that I will not be followed or harassed.
- I can be sure that my children will be given curricula materials that testify to the existence of their race.
- I can be sure that if I ask to talk to "the person in charge" I will be facing a person of my race.
- I can be sure if I need legal or medical help my race will not act against me.

Being culturally aware of white privilege makes one newly accountable. As stated by McIntosh, "having described it, what will I do to lessen or end it?"

In commenting on cultural awareness and racism, Beer (1998) states that "all of us carry stereotypes and prejudices--it is in the air we breathe." She further adds that "we can challenge and control our prejudices and biases to some extent...however, what we can't easily change is the system we are part of, the fact that our positional identity gives us a relative advantage or disadvantage whether we seek to have it or not."

The process of gaining cultural awareness is an important first step in one's journey towards cultural competence. Pedersen (1988) suggests the following techniques to stimulate cultural awareness: (1) experiential exercises (role plays, role reversals, simulations); (2) field trips; (3) guided self-study with a reading list; (4) critical incidents; (5) panel discussions; (6) audio-visual presentations; (7) interviews with consultants and experts; and (8) bicultural observations. Pedersen's goal in this awareness focus is to assist the healthcare professional to become aware of the contrast and conflict between their background and that of the client's cultural background. However, becoming aware of racism and one's prejudices and biases towards other cultures doesn't insure the development of culturally responsive interventions (Campinha-Bacote, 1998). Healthcare professionals must develop other needed components of cultural competency.

CHAPTER 4

Cultural Knowledge

*"There are more differences within cultural groups
than across cultural groups..."*

Campinha-Bacote

*Cultural knowledge is the process of seeking and obtaining a sound
educational base about culturally diverse groups* (Campinha-Bacote 1998).
In obtaining this cultural knowledge, the healthcare professional must focus
on the integration of three specific issues: health-related beliefs, practices
and cultural values; disease incidence and prevalence; and treatment
efficacy (Lavizzo-Mourey, 1996).

Obtaining knowledge regarding the client's health-related beliefs,
practices and values necessitates an understanding of their worldview. One
of the most influential factors for understanding an individual's behavior
is to understand their worldview. An individual's worldview becomes
the foundation for all actions and interpretations (Galanti, 1991).
Nichols' (1987) theoretical model, The Philosophical Aspects of Cultural
Differences, asserts that a cultural groups' worldview includes axiology,
epistemology, logic and process. *Axiology* is what a culture values the
highest. Nichols contends that for some African Americans, the highest
value lies in interpersonal relationships between persons; while some
European Americans' highest value lies in the acquisition of objects or what
we would refer to as materialism. *Epistemology* refers to how a cultural
group comes to know truth or knowledge. For example, some African
Americans come to knowledge affectively, or through feelings. *Logic* refers
to a cultural group's nature of reasoning, while *process* refers to a cultural
group's view of the nature of relationships in the world.

Disease incidence and prevalence is the second issue healthcare
professionals must address when obtaining cultural knowledge. Disease

incidence varies among ethnic groups and healthcare professionals that do not have accurate epidemological data to guide decisions about treatment, health education, screening, and treatment programs may have a negative impact on healthcare outcomes. Common diseases and health conditions found among ethnic groups are reflected in the following list:

Chinese Americans
Hepatitis B
Tuberculosis
Diabetes mellitus
Pancreatic cancer in women

Arab Americans
Sickle cell anemia
Thalassemias
Familial hypercholesterolemia
Mediterranean fever

Jewish Americans
Genetic disorders (e.g., Tay-Sachs disease, Gaucher's disease, Niemann-Pick disease, Bloom's syndrome, and Riely-Day syndrome)
Inflammatory bowel disease
Karposi's sarcoma in men of Ashkenazi descent

Mexican Americans
Cancer
Alcoholism and drug abuse
Diabetes Mellitus
Dental diseases

Navajo Indians
Severe combined immunodeficiency syndrome, unrelated to AIDS
Genetically prone blindness
Diabetes Mellitus
Navajo neuropathy
Albinism

Cultural Knowledge

In addition to these diseases and health conditions found among ethnic
groups, some examples of health disparities prevalent among the African
American population are:

1. African American children are three times more likely to be
   hospitalized for asthma than White children.
2. Of the 18,361 reported tuberculosis cases (TB) in the United States
   in 1998, a majority occurred among minorities. While African
   Americans represent 12.8% of the U.S. population, they accounted
   for 31.8 % of the cases.
3. Colerectal cancer is the third most common cancer among
   African Americans.

Treatment efficacy is the third issue to address in the process of obtaining
cultural knowledge. This involves obtaining knowledge in such areas as
ethnic pharmacology. Ethnic pharmacology is the study of variations in
drug metabolism among ethnic groups. However, healthcare professionals
must be aware of the current controversy surrounding the topic of ethnic
pharmacology.

Schwartz (2001) maintains that ethnic pharmacology is a form of racial
profiling, for genome studies clearly demonstrate that although we are
phenotypically different, we are more genotypically similar across ethnic and
racial groups. In contrast, Satel (2000) asserts that although race is a rough
biological classification, healthcare professionals must not be blind to its
clinical application. Satel further adds that much of medicine is a guessing
game and race sometimes provides an invaluable clue. Considering these
above viewpoints, it is recommended that healthcare professionals use
caution when obtaining and applying knowledge of ethnic pharmacology.
Healthcare professionals must be aware of possible clinical applications
of this field of study, while at the same time demonstrating a respect for
individual differences and similarities across racial groups.

Cultural Knowledge

In clinically applying the field of ethnic pharmacology, healthcare professionals must be knowledgeable of the factors involved in determining responses to a specific drug among ethnic groups. These factors include environmental concerns, the cultural beliefs and practices of both client and healthcare professional, genetics, and generic drug substitution. One *environmental factor* noted among ethnic groups is diet. Medications that require fat in order to be absorbed, such as griseofulvin (an antifungal agent), are often more effective in ethnic groups who main a high-fat diet. Malnutrition can also influence drug response. Protein, vitamin and mineral deficiencies can hamper the function of metabolic enzymes which can alter the body's ability to absorb or eliminate a drug.

An example of a *cultural* factor that can influence drug response in ethnic groups is the client's use of herbs. Ethnopharmacology, also called phytomedicine, is the study of herbs and their medicinal properties. Many cultural groups' values, beliefs and practices include the use herbs to treat illnesses and maintain health, which may interfere with the healthcare professionals' treatment plan. Eisenberg et. al (1998) conducted a large scale study in which they found 15 million adults were at risk for drug-herb interaction. Other studies reveal that approximately 40% of clients enrolled in health maintenance organizations (HMOs) were on herbs without their primary care provider's knowledge (Eisenberg et. al, 1993).

Another *cultural* factor that can effect drug response among ethnic groups is the healthcare professional's biases and prejudices toward culturally diverse groups. This prejudice can lead to misdiagnosis and over-medication. DelBello et. al (1999) found in a study with adolescents that although there were no differences in psychotic symptoms among African Americans and Caucasians, African American adolescents still received more antipsychotic medications. There are several possible explanations for this discrepancy, however, DelBello cites that one possibility is that clinicians perceived African Americans to be more aggressive and more psychotic and thus prescribed the antipsychotic. Similarly, studies conducted by Lawson (1999), Strakowski et. al (1996), and Strickland et. al (1995) also found that African Americans were more likely to be prescribed antipsychotics as well as more likely to be diagnosed with schizophrenia.

Genetics also play a role in drug response among ethnic groups. The cytochrome P450 system contains over 200 genetically determined enzymes known to regulate drug metabolism. Certain types of genetic variations (allele frequencies) of importance in the metabolism of drugs are more common in some ethnic groups than others. For example, half of the Chinese and Japanese populations have a polymorphism of the gene encoding the enzyme alcohol dehydrogenase 2, resulting in an inactive variant of that enzyme that has been associated with Asian alcohol hypersensitivity and the risk for esophageal cancer (Takeshita, 2000). Caucasian or African populations rarely show this isozyme variation.

Therapeutic ranges of lithium can also differ among ethnic groups. Lin, Poland, & Lesser (1986) reported that the therapeutic range of lithium for manic patients in Japan and Taiwan to be 0.4 - 0.8 mEq/L, as compared to 0.6 - 1.2 mEq/L for patients in the United States. In another research study, Schaeffeler et. al (2001) found that a genetic mutation may make certain antiretroviral treatments less effective in Africans and African Americans.

Generic substitution of a trade drug can be an issue for certain ethnic groups. While 10% of the active drug component of a generic drug can differ, there is a greater range allowed in the filler. Lactose, a common filler constituent, may be relied on to a greater degree and may cause unpleasant side effects in susceptible ethnic populations (Levy, 1993). Certain insurance company's prescribing formulary may not take this factor into account.

In addition to treatment efficacy, cultural knowledge is needed in the area of diagnostic clarity among cultural groups. Diagnostic clarity includes the role of the healthcare professional and their ability to maintain diagnostic objectivity in cross-cultural situations. The Surgeon General's Report on Mental Health states that persons from racial and ethnic groups are often misdiagnosed within mental health systems (U.S. Department of Health and Human Services, 2001). Therefore, diagnostic clarity becomes an important factor to consider when providing psychiatric and mental health care to racial and ethnic groups, for it can be confounded by differences in behavioral expressions among various cultural groups.

The select expression of an illness by a culture is referred to as a culture-bound illness or syndrome. The healthcare professional must become knowledgeable of culture-bound illnesses to maintain diagnostic clarity and prevent potential misdiagnosis among cultural groups. Leff (1981) defines culture-bound syndromes as features of an illness that vary from culture to culture. Susto (fright) and mal ojo (evil eye) are two culture-bound syndromes noted in some Hispanic/Latino populations. *Susto*, or soul loss, is the belief that a frightening experience can cause illness. When this fright occurs, it is believed that the soul of the victim has been captured by spirits. Symptoms include anorexia, listless, apathy and withdrawal (Harwood, 1981). If not aware of this culture-bound illness, healthcare professionals may misdiagnosis susto as clinical depression. This misdiagnosis can further lead to inappropriate treatment. *Mal ojo* embodies the belief that social relations contain dangers to an individual. It is stated that women and children are more susceptible to this illness because they are weaker. The belief is that a strong person with "vista Fuerte" (strong vision) can exert a negative power over the weaker person causing them to become ill. Symptoms such as fevers, rashes, nervousness and irritability appear abruptly.

Since mal ojo and susto, as well as other culture-bound illnesses, can closely mimic psychopathology, there is a serious concern for misdiagnosis among cultural groups. In response to this concern, the Diagnostic and Statistical

Cultural Knowledge

Manual of Mental Disorders (DSM-IV, 1994) proposed an outline for a
systematic evaluation of the impact of the client's cultural context. This
outline includes assessment of the cultural identity of the client, cultural
explanations of the client's illness, cultural elements of the relationship
between the client and the healthcare professional, cultural factors related
to the psychosocial environment and levels of functioning, and the overall
cultural assessment for diagnostic care. The DSM-IV also provides
healthcare professionals with a glossary list of best-studied cultural-bound
syndromes and idioms of distress that one may encounter during cross-
cultural assessments.

In obtaining cultural knowledge it is also important to understand the
different interacting styles found within cultural groups. Bell & Evans
(1981) assert that there are four distinctive interacting style; acculturated,
culturally-immersed, traditional, and bicultural. The *acculturated*
interpersonal style is when a client from a culturally diverse group makes a
conscious or unconscious decision to reject the values, beliefs, practices
and general behaviors associated with his/her own cultural group. In
contrast, the *culturally-immersed* client rejects all values, except those held
by their cultural group. These clients are often labeled as militant or
difficult. This client becomes immersed in his/her culture as a survival
mechanism. The *traditional* interpersonal style is noted when the client
neither rejects nor accepts their cultural identity. They do not disclose
information about their cultural practices. Finally, the *bicultural* interacting
style demonstrates the pride that a client has for their history and cultural traditions,
while still feeling connected and comfortable in the mainstream world. These
clients live in both worlds; but at an emotional expense. Culturally diverse clients
who choose to operate under a bicultural interacting style take on the risk of being
negatively labeled by their own cultural group as "trying to act White."
African Americans operating in a bicultural interacting style are referred to
as "Oreos" - black on the outside, but white on the inside; while Native

Cultural Knowledge

Americans are called "apples" - red on the outside, but white on the inside. Similarly, Hispanics/Latinos are labeled as "coconuts" by their own cultural group - brown on the outside, but white on the inside and Asians are referred to as "bananas" - yellow on the outside, but white on the inside. It is important to understand these four interacting styles of culturally diverse groups when rendering care, for an acculturated client may be offended by your offer of culturally relevant services, while the culturally-immersed client will demand these services.

In obtaining cultural knowledge, it is critical to remember the concept of intra-cultural variation; there is more variation within cultural groups than across cultural groups. No individual is a stereotype of one's culture of origin, but rather a unique blend of the diversity found within each culture, an accumulation of life experiences, and the process of acculturation to other cultures. In addition, it is important to keep in mind that cultures are constantly evolving and no healthcare professional can hope to be completely familiar with the health beliefs and practices of all their clients, nor can clients realistically expect such encyclopedia awareness from the healthcare professional (Recommendations from the Minnesota Public Health Associations Immigrant Health Task Force, 1996). Healthcare professionals cannot solely rely on textbooks and websites for cultural knowledge. They must also develop the skill necessary to obtain cultural knowledge directly from their client. Therefore, the healthcare professional must develop the skill to conduct a cultural assessment with each client.

CHAPTER 5

Cultural Skill

*"Everyone needs a cultural assessment; not just
people who look like they need one..."*

Campinha-Bacote

*Cultural skill is the ability to collect relevant cultural data regarding the
client's presenting problem as well as accurately perform a culturally-based,
physical assessment* (Campinha-Bacote, 1998). This process involves
learning the skills of how to conduct a cultural assessment and perform
culturally-based physical assessments. Leininger (1978) defines a cultural
assessment as a "systematic appraisal or examination of individuals,
groups, and communities as to their cultural beliefs, values and practices to
determine explicit needs and intervention practices within the context of the
people being served" (pp. 85-86). The literature is saturated with cultural
assessment tools, frameworks and mnemonics that can assist healthcare
professionals in conducting a cultural assessment.

I will present a brief overview of selected cultural assessment tools that can
be useful across healthcare disciplines and specialties. My intent is to provide
healthcare professionals with a wide selection of cultural questions, mnemonics,
domains and/or phenomena that can be integrated into their existing health
history or assessment form. I refer to this process as the Integrated Model
Approach to Conducting Cultural Assessments (Campinha-Bacote 1998),
which consists of the following steps: (1) review several cultural assessment
tools; (2) consider your discipline's and speciality's goal in conducting an

assessment; (3) consider your personal assets and liabilities as an interviewer; and (4) incorporate selected questions from specific cultural assessment tools that will augment your existing assessment form to yield culturally relevant data. If a cultural assessment is conducted in this manner, culture is not singled-out, but rather appropriately incorporated into the client's overall assessment. As stated by Osler, "It is more important to know what kind of patient has a disease than what kind of disease a patient has."

There are several cultural assessment tools that describe domains or phenomena to be considered when assessing a client's cultural background (Leininger, 1978; Purnell, 1998; Giger & Davidhizar, 1999). Purnell (1998) developed an organizing framework consisting of 12 domains which are common to all cultures:

1. Overview, inhabited localities and topography
2. Communication
3. Family roles and organization
4. Workforce issues
5. Biocultural ecology
6. High-risk health behaviors
7. Nutrition
8. Pregnancy and childbearing
9. Death rituals
10. Spirituality
11. Health-care practices
12. Health-care practitioners

Overview, inhabited localities and topography includes the client's heritage and residence, reasons for migration and associated economic factors, educational status and occupation. The domain of *communication* involves knowing about the client's language and dialect, cultural communication patterns, temporal relationships and format for names. *Workforce issues* relate to the differences and conflicts that occur in the workplace setting. These issues include such factors as degree of assimilation and acculturation and issues related to professional autonomy. *Family roles and organization* require gaining information about family roles and priorities, alternative lifestyles and traditional families, and issues surrounding gender and head of household. *Biocultural ecology* is the specific domain that identifies the client's physical, biological and physiological variations. Examples of these variations are noted in drug metabolism and disease and health conditions. *High-risk health behaviors* include specific high-risk behaviors common among cultural groups. These behaviors may include the use of alcohol, tobacco and recreational drugs. The cultural domain, *nutrition*, includes the client's meaning of food, common food and food rituals, dietary practices for health promotion, and nutritional deficiencies and limitations. The domain, *pregnancy and childrearing practices*, includes obtaining knowledge about the client's culturally sanctioned and unsanctioned fertility practices; views toward pregnancy; and prescriptive, restrictive and taboo practices related to pregnancy, birthing and postpartum. *Death rituals* include how the client views death and euthanasia, rituals to prepare for death and bereavement, and burial practices. The domain of *spirituality* involves more than the client's religious affiliation. Spirituality encompasses religious practices, use of prayer, meaning of life and individual sources of strength, spiritual beliefs and healthcare practices related to these beliefs. *Health-care practices* include health-seeking behaviors and beliefs, responsibility for health-care, folklore practices, barriers to care, cultural responses to health and illness, and beliefs regarding blood transfusions, organ donation and organ transplantation. The final domain of *health-care practitioner* includes the status, use and perceptions of traditional, magicoreligious practitioners, and biomedical healthcare professionals.

Giger and Davidhizar (1999) assert that their Transcultural Assessment Model "provides healthcare professionals with a practical assessment tool for evaluating cultural variables that greatly minimizes the time needed to conduct a comprehensive assessment" (p. 6). These authors contend that culturally diverse care must take into account six cultural phenomena that vary with application and use, yet are evident in all cultural groups: (1) communication, (2) space, (3) social organization, (4) time, (5) environmental control, and (6) biological variation. The variable, *communication*, addresses both verbal and non-verbal communication, while the variable of *space* assesses issues regarding personal boundaries and interpersonal space. *Social organization* includes assessing such information as family structure and religious values, while the phenomenon of *time* refers to not only assessing how the client measures time, but their temporal perspective (past, present or future). *Environmental control* addresses the client's ability to plan activities that control nature. This variable includes the client' health practices. The final variable of *biological variations* includes the client's physical dimensions, enzymatic and genetic existence of diseases specific to their cultural group, and nutritional preferences and deficiencies.

Leininger (1995) encourages healthcare processionals to use her Culture Care Theory, along with her Sunrise Model, to conduct a holistic "culturalological" assessment. The major areas of assessment are worldview and social structure factors which include cultural values, beliefs and practices; religious, philosophical or spiritual beliefs; economic factors; educational beliefs; technology views; kinship and social ties; and political and legal factors. In addition to these areas, Leininger suggests for the healthcare processional to "assess generic folk and professional beliefs, practices and experiences, searching for the client's cultural interpretations or explanations in relation to generic and professional care" (p. 121).

Like Leininger (1995), Kleinman (1980) is also interested in the client's explanation of their illness. He refers to this as the client's Explanatory Model. Explanatory models (EMs) are notions about sickness and its treatment. There are five major questions that EMs seek to explain for illness episodes: (1) etiology, (2) time and mode of onset of symptoms; (3) pathophysiology, (4) course of illness (including both severity and type of sick role), and (5) treatment. Kleinman finds it useful to ask the following open-ended questions in eliciting the details of the client's explanatory model:

1. What do you call your problem? What name does it have?

2. What do you think has caused your problem?

3. Why do you think it started when it did?

4. What do you think your sickness does to you? How
   does it work?

5. How severe is it? Will it have a short or long course?

6. What do you fear the most about your sickness?

7. What are the chief problems your sickness has caused for you?

8. What kind of treatment do you think you should receive? What
   are the most important results you hope to receive from this
   treatment? (p. 106).

To provide ease in conducting a cultural assessment, several authors have developed mnemonic cultural assessment tools (Fong, 1985; Carillo, Green & Betancourt, 1999; Berlin & Fowkes, 1982; Stuart & Lieberman, 1993; Levine, Like, & Gottlieb, 2000). Fong (1985) provides the mnemonic, CONFHER, as a framework for assessing the client's cultural background. CONFHER represents the cultural components of:

C ommunication style
O rientation
N utrition
F amily relationships
H ealth beliefs
E ducation
R eligion

Cultural Skill

Communication involves obtaining information on the client's language and dialect preference as well as nonverbal social customs. *Orientation* refers to the client's cultural identity. Asking the client what cultural group they identify with, allows the client to choose their own cultural orientation, rather than being labeled by the healthcare professional. Orientation also refers to how closely the client adheres to the traditional habits and values of their cultural group. *Nutritional* information can be obtained by asking such questions as: "Are there ethnic foods that you prefer?"; "Are there foods that you are encouraged to eat when sick?"; "Are there foods to be avoided because of your cultural origin, health status, or illness?" Family *relationships* involve assessing how the client defines family and how decisions are made in the family. Questions that can help in eliciting the client's *health beliefs* are: "Do you rely on any self-care or traditional folk medicine practices?"; "How do you explain your illness?"; and "How do you feel about being in the hospital?" *Educational* information can be obtained by assessing such factors as whether or not the client prefers to learn information by receiving printed literature, listening or viewing audio visual learning tools, by using hands-on experiential learning that involves trial and error or by didactic methods. *Religious* data involves the assessment of the client's religious or spiritual preference, beliefs, sacred rites, restrictions, and person that will be involved in their care to provide spiritual and religious comfort.

Stuart & Lieberman (1993) provide healthcare professionals with the mnemonic BATHE, for eliciting the psychological context of the client's presenting problem:

> **B** ackground
>
> **A** ffect
>
> **T** rouble
>
> **H** andling
>
> **E** mpathy

Cultural Skill

To assess the *background* of the problem, a question such as, "W
going on in your life?," elicits the context of the client's visit. *Affect c*
assessed by asking, "How do you feel about what's going on?" or "What is
your mood?" for it allows the client to label his current feeling state. The
question, "What about the situation *troubles* you the most?" helps both the
healthcare professional and client to focus and may bring out the symbolic
significance of the problem or illness. It is also important to assess how the
client is *handling* the problem, for it will give an assessment of functioning
and provides direction for intervention. Finally, offering *empathy* to the
client legitimizes their feelings and provides psychological support.

Berlin and Fowkes (1982) suggest the mnemonic, LEARN, in conducting
a cultural assessment. This mnemonic represents the following 5 steps:

> **L** isten
>
> **E** xplain
>
> **A** cknowledge
>
> **R** ecommend
>
> **N** egotiate

The first step is to *listen* to the client's perception of their presenting
problem. The healthcare professional then *explains* their perception of the
client's problem, whether it be physiological, psychological, spiritual, or
cultural. The next step is to *acknowledge* the similarities and
differences between the two perceptions. At times it is easier for the
healthcare professional to acknowledge cultural differences, than to
acknowledge and focus on the similarities that they have in common. In
order to provide a culturally relevant treatment regime, it is important to
recognize differences, but build on similarities. The third step focuses on
recommendations, which must involve the client. Finally, the healthcare

professional is to *negotiate* a treatment plan, considering that it is beneficial to incorporate selected aspects of the client's culture in providing culturally competent care.

Levine, Like, & Gottlieb (2000) suggest still another mnemonic tool-ETHNIC. ETHNIC represents:

> **E** xplanation
>
> **T** reatment
>
> **H** ealers
>
> **N** egotiate
>
> **I** ntervention
>
> **C** ollaboration

Using this mnemonic model, the healthcare professional is to begin by having the client *explain* their problem. Similar to Kleinman's (1980) explanatory model, the healthcare professional is trying to elicit the client's explanation of the problem. If the client cannot offer an explanation, ask what most concerns them about their problem. It is also important to ask the client what kinds of *treatments* they have tried for their problem. This may include the use of vitamins, herbs and home remedies. Next, the healthcare professional is to assess if the client has sought advice from alternative or folk *healers*, friends, or other individuals who are not healthcare professionals. The healthcare professional then *negotiates*, in an attempt to find an option that will be mutually acceptable to both healthcare professional and client. The healthcare professional determines an *intervention* which may incorporate alternate treatments. It is important to *collaborate* with the client, family members, other healthcare professionals, healers and community resources during all the phases of the assessment.

Due to the rapidly changing demographics of our growing multicultural world, healthcare professionals will encounter clients that may have recently

migrated to the United States or who are refugees. Jacobsen (1988) refers
to these clients as ethnoculturally translocated clients. Existing cultural
assessment tools may not be appropriate for these clients and Jacobsen
proposes a five stage assessment tool. In stage I, the healthcare professional
obtains information on the client's ethnocultural heritage, such as the
culture of origin for both maternal and paternal lines of the client's family.
Stage II requires the healthcare professional to assess the circumstances
leading to the client's ethno-cultural translocation(s). Stages III and IV
assess the client's intellectual and emotional perception of the development
of the family's niche in society since translocation, as well as the client's
view of their cultural adjustment as an individual. The final stage addresses
information regarding the healthcare professional's ethno-cultural
background and areas of overlap or differences.

As earlier stated in the definition of cultural skill, healthcare professionals
also need to develop cultural skill when performing a physical assessment on
culturally diverse clients. The healthcare professional should know how a
client's physical, biological and physiological variations influence the ability
to conduct an accurate and appropriate physical evaluation (Purnell, 1998;
Bloch, 1983). One common example is the occurrence of inverted T waves
in the precordial leads of the electrocardiogram found among African
American males (Giger & Davidhizar, 1999). Although an abnormal finding
in other racial groups, this finding is a normal variation in the African
American population.

In performing a culturally-based physical assessment, Bloch (1983)
encourages healthcare professionals to internally ask such questions as:
"Does the client have ethnic variations in anatomical characteristics? (e.g. many
Vietnamese children are commonly small by American standards, not fitting
the published growth curves); "Does ethnic-anatomical characteristics
affect physical evaluations?"; "Are there distinct growth and developmental
characteristics that vary with a client's ethnic background?" and "How does

skin color variation influence assessment of skin color changes and its relationship to the disease process?"

The skin pigmentation of African American clients changes the presentation of many common skin manifestations. Therefore, pallor, localized hyperpigmentation lesions, petechiae, erythema, and ecchymosis, must be interpreted differently in dark-skinned clients. For example, inflammation is often missed in clients with dark skin and may not be diagnosed until the flare becomes severe. Palpation must be used in localizing warmth, induration, and tightness of the skin in early cases. Lesions of Karposi's sacoma and Basillary angiomatosis can be overlooked and confused with other lesions in dark-skinned clients (McNeil, Campinha-Bacote, & Vample, 2002). A well-lighted examination with palpation of all suspected lesions is important in these clients.

Assessing jaundice in Asian clients is more easily determined by assessing sclera, the palm of their hands and the soles of their feet, rather than relying on the change in skin color. Parreno's (1977) Skin Color Scale for Assessing Normal Skin Pigmentation in Asians is a useful tool when conducting physical assessments on Asians.

Assessing cyanosis and blood oxygenation levels are also different in dark-skinned clients than in light-skinned clients. Some dark-skinned clients from the Mediterranean region may have very blue lips, which may give a false impression of cyanosis. Healthcare professionals should examine the oral mucosa and capillary refill at the nail bed when assessing anemia in dark-skinned clients (Purnell & Paulanka, 1998). Purnell & Paulanka (1998) offer the following guidelines for assessing skin variations: 1) establish a baseline color (ask a family member); 2) use direct sunlight if possible; 3) observe areas with the least amount of pigment; 4) palpate for rashes; and 5) compare skin in corresponding areas.

Conducting a cultural assessment is more than selecting a tool and asking the client questions listed on the tool, it requires cultural skill. The healthcare professional's approach must be done in a culturally sensitive manner. Buchwald et. al (1994) suggest several techniques for eliciting cultural content from the client in a sensitive manner. It is suggested that healthcare professionals listen with interest and remain non-judgemental about what they hear. For example, an African American family may openly tell the healthcare professional that they use physical punishment to discipline their children. The African American family's focus on physical forms of discipline may initially present controversial and ethical concerns for the healthcare professional (Campinha-Bacote & Ferguson, 1991). However, the healthcare professional must remain non-judgemental and not assume that child abuse is occurring within the family system. It is important to conduct a culturally sensitive assessment to assess for child abuse. The healthcare professional may find out that this form of discipline is a characteristic of a functional, and appropriate disciplinary behavior of these caring African American parents. As stated by McGoldrick (1982), strict discipline is a way in which some African American parents protect their children from severe consequences of acting-out behavior.

Healthcare professionals can use other techniques in eliciting cultural information in a culturally sensitive manner. For example, the healthcare professional may want to develop alternative styles of inquiry by adopting a less direct and more conversational approach to assessing the client's background. Healthcare professionals may consider a conversational remark such as, "Tell me about yourself and your family." Another technique is to frame questions in the context of other clients or the client's family. For example, a healthcare professional can say, "I know another client who had such and such an idea of what was wrong. Do you think that?" or "What does your mother think is causing your problem?" Attributing explanations to another person can help clients disclose health beliefs and practices that they may feel initially uncomfortable expressing (Buchwald et. al, 1994).

Cultural Skill

Although there are several techniques available to assist healthcare professionals in eliciting cultural information in a culturally sensitive manner, the healthcare professional may still feel awkward in obtaining this information. This feeling is not unusual, for in learning how to conduct a cultural assessment healthcare professionals pass through several levels of skill acquisition. The Dreyfus Model is a helpful framework for understanding the levels of skill acquisition when conducting a cultural assessment (Dreyfus and Dreyfus, 1980). Although Stuart Dreyfus and Hubert Dreyfus developed their model of skill acquisition based upon their study of chess players and airline pilots, Benner (1984) has applied the Dreyfus Model of skill acquisition to nursing. I will further expand this model of skill acquisition to healthcare professionals conducting a cultural assessment.

The Dreyfus Model (1980) asserts that individuals pass through five levels of proficiency in skill acquisition: novice, advanced beginner, competent, proficient, and expert. The *novice* healthcare professional has little understanding of how to conduct a cultural assessment. They possess the "know that" knowledge but not the "know how" knowledge. They "know that" a cultural assessment should be done on each client, but do not "know how" to conduct it in an effective manner. The *advanced beginner* demonstrates marginally acceptable performance in conducting a cultural assessment and has dealt with enough real situations to recognize meaningful components of the assessment. The novice and advanced beginner take in little of the situation and primarily focus on the rules they were taught when conducting a cultural assessment. The third level of skill acquisition is competence. The *competent* healthcare professional usually has two or three years of experience of conducting cultural assessments with culturally diverse populations. This healthcare professional recognizes what information is to be considered most important and what information is to be ignored. However, the competent healthcare professional lacks the speed and flexibility of the proficient healthcare professional. The *proficient* healthcare professional has worked three to five years with culturally diverse clients. They perceive the information gained from the cultural assessment in a holistic manner, rather than in terms of specific aspects of the presenting problem. At this level of skill acquisition, the healthcare professional is able to hone in on accurate regions of the client's problem in regard to cultural implications. Finally, the *expert* healthcare professional does not rely on specific rules to gain information from the client. This healthcare professional has an enormous background of experience with culturally diverse populations and has developed an intuitive grasp of how to conduct a cultural assessment in an effective manner. They are able to listen to the client and obtain relevant information. When asked by colleagues why they may ask a question in a particular way, the expert healthcare professional will remark, "Because it feels right."

It is important to realize that "every client deserves a cultural assessment, not just clients who look like they need a cultural assessment" (Campinha-Bacote, 1998). Many times, healthcare professionals may use the last name of the client or the client's physical appearance as a justification to conduct a cultural assessment. This is unacceptable, for the basic premise of a cultural assessment is that clients have a right to have their values, beliefs, and practices understood, respected and incorporated into their care (Leininger, 1978). This includes *all* clients. Data obtained from a cultural assessment will allow healthcare professionals to formulate a mutually acceptable and culturally relevant treatment plan. This assessment data will also prevent possible misdiagnosis of the client's behavior. To acquire a skill level of expertise when conducting a cultural assessment, it is necessary to have many encounters with clients. Therefore, cultural encounters are a critical component of becoming culturally competent.

CHAPTER 6

Cultural Encounters

"Our first task in approaching a people, another culture, another religion is to take off our shoes; for the ground we are approaching is holy..."

Columbian Fathers

Cultural encounter is the process which encourages the healthcare professional to directly engage in face-to-face interactions with clients from culturally diverse backgrounds (Campinha-Bacote, 1998). Interacting directly with clients from diverse cultural groups will refine or modify one's existing beliefs about a cultural group and will prevent stereotyping. However, healthcare professionals must be cautious and recognize that by only interacting with three or four members from a specific ethnic group, does not make one an expert on that group. It is possible that these three or four individuals may or may not truly represent the stated beliefs, values, practices of the specific cultural group which the healthcare professional has encountered.

Clark, Hewson & Fry (1996) suggest the mnemonic, PEARLS, as a framework for interacting with clients. PEARLS represents the culturally sensitive communication skills of partnership, empathy, apology, respect, legitimization and support. Healthcare professionals may want to incorporate the following suggested comments into their cultural encounters to reflect what these authors call, "PEARLS of Communication:"

P artnership: "Let's tackle this together."
E mpathy: "That sounds difficult."
A pologize: "I apologize for the wait."
R espect: "Help me understand."
L egitimization: "I hear you."
S upport: "Here is my card, please call if..."

Cultural Encounters

Every encounter should be considered a cultural encounter, for healthcare professionals themselves can be viewed as a cultural group with unique values, beliefs, practices and language. Some explicit rules from the American healthcare professional culture may be quite foreign to clients of other cultures. Dube', Goldman, & Monroe (1998) give the following examples:

- Clients must make appointments to be seen.
- Clients see a healthcare professional when they are
  not sick (well visits for preventive care).
- Clients must disrobe and wear a gown or a drape.
- Healthcare professionals must be credentialed.

Cultural encounters can become challenging when the client does not speak English. Therefore, cultural encounters require an assessment of the client's linguistic needs. Using a formally trained medical interpreter, either on site or via telephone, is required and necessary to facilitate accurate communication during the encounter. The use of untrained interpreters, friends or family members may pose a problem due to their lack of knowledge regarding medical terminology and disease entities. This situation is heightened when children are used as interpreters. One glaring example is noted in the case of the obstetrical healthcare professional who needed to communicate to her client that she was going to deliver a still birth. The healthcare professional did not speak Spanish and used the client's 6 year old daughter to interpret to the mother that the baby was dead. We can clearly see in this tragic case that a trained medical interpreter was needed. In 1998, The Office of Civil Rights issued a National Guidance Memorandum regarding the care of clients who have limited English proficiency and provided guidance on working with medical interpreters.

Cultural Encounters

Like (2000) suggests that the mnemonic TRANSLATE, be used as a guiding framework when working with medical interpreters:

T rust
R oles
A dvocacy
N on-judgemental attitude
S etting
L anguage
A ccuracy
T ime
E thical issues

Like developed this model based on the works of Kraufert & Putsh (1997). This mnemonic addresses the issues of trust, roles, advocacy, non-judgemental attitude, setting, language, accuracy, time and ethical issues. The healthcare professional must address how *trust* will be developed in the client-interpreter relationship as well as in the relationship with the client's family and other healthcare professionals. The *role* or roles that the medical interpreter will play in the clinical care process must also be considered. For example, will the interpreter serve as a language interpreter, culture broker/ informant, culture broker/ interpreter of biomedical culture, or as an advocate? *Advocacy* issues include asking such questions as, "How will advocacy and support for the client and family care occur?" and "How will power and loyalty issues be handled?" The healthcare professional should also consider how a *non-judgemental attitude* will be maintained during this clinical encounter and how his/her personal attitude, values beliefs and biases are to be dealt with. The *setting* is important and the healthcare professional needs to be apprised of where and how the medical interpretation will occur during health care. The healthcare professional must ask how *linguistic* appropriateness and competence will be assessed; how knowledge and information will be exchanged in an *accurate*, thorough, and complete manner; how *time* will be managed; and how confidentiality and other *ethical* issues will be handled during this encounter.

All encounters may not be face-to-face interactions. Telephonic communication has become a cost-effective way of providing primary, secondary and tertiary services to clients. However, verbal communication via the telephone elicits challenges for healthcare professionals that is not experienced in face-to-face encounters. The healthcare professionals must rely solely on verbal communication, without the advantage of relating this verbal communication to the cultural context of the client's non-verbal behavior (facial gestures, body movements, etc.). Based on my model of cultural competence, I developed a checklist for healthcare professionals to consider during telephonic communications with clients. This checklist considers attitudes, knowledge and skills needed for effective telephonic communication (Appendix C).

In addition to telephonic encounters, healthcare professionals may be facing other forms of non-face-to-face cultural encounters. The advent of technology has created such encounters as the Internet, World Wide Web and E-mail communication. These encounters will challenge healthcare professionals to develop culturally responsive approaches when using these forms of technology. The goals of cultural encounters are to generate a wide variety of responses and to send and receive both verbal and nonverbal communication accurately and appropriately in each culturally different context (adapted from Sue et. al, 1982).

CHAPTER 7

Application Of The Model

*"Don't fear mistakes - only fear the absence of creative,
constructive and corrective responses to these mistakes..."*

Rolf Kerr

*The Process of Cultural Competence in the Delivery of Healthcare
Services,* is a model of cultural competence for all healthcare professionals,
in all healthcare settings and in all areas of practice. It has been suggested
as a model for conducting culturally sensitive research (Campinha-Bacote
& Padgett, 1995); a model for clinical competence in specialty areas such
as psychiatric care, rehabilitation, community services and home care
(Campinha-Bacote, 2002; Campinha-Bacote, 2001; Campinha-Bacote,
1999; Campinha-Bacote & Munoz, 2001; Campinha-Bacote & Narayan,
2000); an educational model for health professions (Campinha-Bacote,
Yahle & Langerkamp, 1996); a framework for policy development
(Campinha-Bacote & Ferguson, 1997); a model for management
and administration (Campinha-Bacote, 1996); and as a guideline for
managed care organizations (Campinha- Bacote & Campinha-Bacote, 1999).
The following article provides an example of how this model can be applied
to the clinical area of rehabilitation.

A Model of Practice to Address Cultural Competence in Rehabilitation Nursing

Josepha Campinha-Bacote, PhD, APRN, BC, CNS, CTN, FAAN
Reprinted from the <u>Rehabilitation Nursing</u> (2001), Volume 26, Issue 1, pages 8-11.

A position statement developed by the Association of Rehabilitation Nurses (ARN), Appropriate Inclusion of Rehabilitation Nurses Wherever Rehabilitation is Provided, stated that nurses are an essential part of a client's rehabilitation because they provide holistic care and "attend to the full range of human experiences and responses to health and illness" (Association of Rehabilitation Nurses, 1996, p.1). Rehabilitation nurses must become strongly aware of the role that culture plays in this process. This article presents a conceptual model of practice with which to address cultural competence in rehabilitation nursing. The model's constructs of cultural awareness, cultural knowledge, cultural encounters, cultural skill, and cultural desire are discussed. Examples from the field of rehabilitation nursing are presented in the discussion of these constructs.

Introduction

When the issue of cultural competence in rehabilitation nursing is addressed, it is essential to comprehend the concept of culture and its relationship to the rehabilitation process. Banja (1996) asserted, "rehabilitation begins in the mind" (p. 279). If this assertion is correct, one must appreciate the many ways that cultural beliefs affect the rehabilitation process, for "culture is tightly interwoven into the life of man and continually pervades his thinking,

actions, feelings and particularly his health state" (Leininger, 1967, p. 37).
A position statement developed by the Association of Rehabilitation
Nurses (ARN), Appropriate Inclusion of Rehabilitation Nurses Wherever
Rehabilitation is Provided, stated that nurses are an essential part of a client's
rehabilitation because they provide holistic care and "attend to the full range
of human experiences and responses to health and illness" (ARN, 1996,
p.1). Consequently, rehabilitation nurses must address the need for cultural
competence in this process. This article provides rehabilitation nurses with a
model of cultural competence that will allow them to begin this process.

The Cultural Competence Model
Campinha-Bacote (1998a) defined the cultural competence in the delivery of
healthcare services model as "the process in which the healthcare provider
continuously strives to achieve the ability to effectively work within the
cultural context of a client, individual, family, or community" (p. 6). This
process requires nurses to see themselves as becoming culturally competent,
rather than being culturally competent. This model views cultural awareness,
cultural knowledge, cultural encounters, cultural skill, and cultural desire as
the five essential constructs of cultural competence. These five constructs
have an interdependent relationship with one another and no matter where
the nurse enters into this process, all five constructs must eventually be
experienced, addressed, or both. Nurses can work on any one of these
constructs to improve the balance of all five. However, it is the intersection
of these constructs that truly depicts the process of cultural competence
(Figure 1). The cultural competence model is complex, multivariate, and
dynamic and reflects the complexity of the actual cyclic process of becoming
culturally competent. To help nurses understand this model, each construct
will be defined, discussed, and illustrated using examples from the field of
rehabilitation nursing.

Application of the Model

Cultural awareness: *Cultural awareness* is the process through which the nurse becomes respectful, appreciative, and sensitive to the values, beliefs, lifeways, practices and problem-solving strategies of a client's culture. This process involves a continual examination of one's own prejudices and biases about other cultures and an in-depth exploration of one's own cultural background. Cultural awareness can further be described as a process of "cultural humility": the lifelong commitment to self-evaluation and critique regarding one's level of cultural awareness (Tervalon & Murray-Garcia, 1998). It may be useful to view cultural awareness along a continuum that ranges from ethnocentrism to ethnorelativism to better understand it.

Ethnocentrism reflects a person's total unawareness that others do not share the same worldview that he or she has. One assumes that his or her values, beliefs, and practices are the only and the correct way to view the world. Without being aware of the influence of one's own cultural values, there is a risk that a nurse may engage in *cultural imposition*, which is the tendency to impose one's beliefs, values, practices, and patterns of behavior upon another culture (Leininger, 1978). Cultural imposition in rehabilitation, for example, may be noted in the area of pain management. Although pain is a universal human experience, nurses are challenged to consider diverse pain modes while working with patients and to strive to interpret pain behavior and meaning from the patient's perspective (Leininger, 1995). For example, some African Americans believe that suffering and pain are inevitable and must be endured (Campinha-Bacote, 1998b), whereas some Arabs regard pain as unpleasant and something to be controlled (Reizan & Meleis, 1986). Cultural imposition also may result in noncompliance. Noncompliance is not a patient problem, but rather reflects the nurse's failure to provide culturally responsive care that incorporates the patient's worldview.

In contrast, ethnorelativism reflects an attitude of nurses who value, respect, and integrate cultural differences into their practices. These nurses do not fear cultural differences and are aware of their attitudes about specific cultural groups. However, becoming aware of one's prejudices and biases about other cultures does not ensure the development of culturally responsive interventions. Nurses must move beyond cultural awareness and develop other needed components of cultural competency.

Cultural knowledge: One of the most important requirements for understanding patient behavior is to have an understanding of the patient's worldview. *Cultural knowledge* results from the process of seeking and obtaining a sound educational foundation about the worldviews of different cultures. A person's worldview explains the value and meaning of his or her life events. Patients in rehabilitation search for the meaning of their illness or disability. It is their worldview that deeply influences what meaning they attach to their health, illness, and disability, as well as what they should do when they become ill or disabled. Should individuals go through rehabilitation, have surgery, become resigned to their illness, do penance, or start a new life? How should they and others act and relate in the presence of illness or disability (Banja, 1996)? The fields of transcultural nursing, medical anthropology, transcultural medicine, cultural anthropology, cross-cultural psychology, and sociology are some of the disciplines that can provide rehabilitation nurses with this educational foundation. Campinha-Bacote (1998a) and Purnell and Paulanka (1998) identified four stages in the process of obtaining cultural knowledge:

1. *Unconscious incompetence* is identified as an individual being unaware that he or she lacks cultural knowledge. Nurses who are unaware that cultural differences exist between themselves and their patients have unconscious incompetence. Buchwald et al. (1994) refer to this state as the cultural blind spot syndrome. A nurse may exhibit unconscious incompetence in the area of biocultural ecology, which includes the study of biological variations, diseases, and health conditions and the variations in drug metabolism among ethnically diverse patients. Does the rehabilitation nurse have knowledge about the field of ethnic pharmacology or the incidence of specific diseases or risk factors among particular ethnic groups?

Application of the Model

The National Institutes of Health (NIH) "Consensus Statements for the Rehabilitation of Persons with Traumatic Brain Injury" (NIH Consensus Development Panel, 1998) concluded that research is needed in the area of epidemiological studies on the risk factors and the incidence of traumatic brain injury among different ethnic groups.

2. *Conscious incompetence* is the awareness that one lacks knowledge about another culture. This awareness may come from attending workshops on cultural diversity, reading articles or books on the topic, or by having direct cross-cultural experiences with patients from culturally diverse backgrounds. Nurses with this awareness possess "the know that knowledge, but not the know how knowledge" (Campinha-Bacote, 1998a, p. 35). They know that culture plays an important role in the rehabilitation process, but they do not know how to effectively use this knowledge.

3. *Conscious competence* is the intentional act of learning about a patient's culture, verifying generalizations, and providing culturally responsive nursing interventions. However, the consciously competent nurse may experience some discomfort at this level. One possible reason for this discomfort is a fear of not being "politically correct." (Campinha-Bacote, 1998a). Nurses at this level are conscious of the need to do and say the right thing, and at times this need may interfere with effective communication. For example, the consciously competent nurse who wants to use the correct term for a Spanish-speaking patient may think, "Do I use the term Hispanic, Latino, or Chicano?"

4. *Unconscious competence* is the ability to automatically provide culturally congruent care to patients from diverse cultural backgrounds. A nurse who is unconsciously competent interacts naturally with patients from diverse cultures (Campinha-Bacote, 1998a).

Application of the Model

Cultural encounters: Acquiring cultural knowledge requires that one have actual cultural encounters. *Cultural encounter* is the process that encourages nurses to engage directly in cross-cultural interactions with clients from culturally diverse backgrounds. We may believe that because we have studied a specific cultural group or interacted with three or four members from a specific ethnic group, that we are knowledgeable about that group. In fact, those three or four individuals may or may not represent the stated beliefs, values, and practices of that specific cultural group. This is due to intra-ethnic variation, in which there is more variation within a cultural group than across cultural groups. It is important to interact directly with patients from diverse cultural groups to refine or modify one's beliefs about those groups. Face-to-face encounters help prevent possible stereotyping.

The goals of cultural encounters are to (a) generate a wide variety of verbal responses and (b) send and receive verbal and nonverbal messages accurately and appropriately in each culturally different context (Sue et al., 1982). However, cultural encounters can be difficult and uncomfortable. Nurses must realize that their good intentions and their usual nonverbal communication style may sometimes be interpreted as offensive and insulting to a specific cultural group. For example, if a nurse wants to give a patient a positive signal during a therapy session, he or she may give the American sign of thumbs up. In Iran, however, a thumb extended up is considered a vulgar gesture. Therefore, nurses must become more sensitive to the meaning of a culture's nonverbal communication, such as eye contact, facial expression, touching, body language, and distancing practices in cross-cultural encounters.

Cultural skill: *Cultural skill* is the ability to collect relevant cultural data about the client's health history and health problem, as well as to accurately perform a culturally-specific physical assessment.

Application of the Model

Leininger (1978) defined a *cultural assessment* as a "systematic appraisal or examination of individuals, groups, and communities as to their cultural beliefs, values, and practices to determine explicit needs and intervention practices within the context of the people being evaluated" (pp. 85–86). The literature offers several assessment tools that nurses can use when conducting a cultural assessment (Berlin & Fowkes, 1982; Giger & Davidhizar, 1999; Kleinman, Eisenburg, & Good, 1978; Purnell, 2000). Banja (1996) suggested the following questions to ask patients during the rehabilitation process:

- How do they understand their illness or disability?

- What do they believe caused the illness?

- What kind of treatment should they receive?

- What does the patient fear (pain, social ostracism, being less of a man or woman)?

- How should the condition or disability be treated by family members?

- If family members continue the rehabilitation effort, how will they react to the disability?

- What are the patient's expectations with regard to the duties and obligations of their family? (pp. 281–282)

The nurse must remember that conducting a cultural assessment is more than selecting a tool and asking the client the questions listed on that tool. The nurse's approach must be done in a culturally sensitive manner. Campinha-Bacote (1995, 1998a) and Buchwald et al. (1994) have identified several techniques for eliciting cultural content from the client in a culturally sensitive manner. One technique requires that the nurse listen to the client with interest and be nonjudgmental.

Application of the Model

For example, Egyptians believe that the evil eye is responsible for personal calamities (Meleis & Meleis, 1998). An Egyptian American patient may tell the nurse that his or her disability or illness is the result of the evil eye and that he or she is using blue beads and religious verses inscribed on charms for protection and to treat the disability. Some nurses may give little credit to such supernatural theories of illness causality and refer to this patient's worldview as primitive, irrational, or superstitious. However, the nurse must remain nonjudgmental and respect the patient's explanation of illness or the cause of his or her disability.

Although the need to conduct a cultural assessment with this Egyptian American patient may be obvious, the nurse must also realize that it is equally important to conduct a cultural assessment with all patients. Every patient has values, beliefs, practices, and lifeways, and every patient needs and deserves a cultural assessment. Cultural assessments are not reserved for patients whose last name may sound different or who may look like they need a cultural assessment (Campinha-Bacote, 1998a).

Cultural skill also is required when doing a physical assessment of ethnically diverse clients. Nurses should know how their clients' physical, biological, and physiological variations influence their own ability to do an accurate and appropriate physical evaluation (Campinha-Bacote, 1998a; Purnell & Paulanka, 1998).

Cultural desire: Cultural desire is the motivation of the nurse to "want to" engage in the process of cultural competence (not the "have to"). Nurses who have cultural awareness, cultural knowledge, and cultural skill, and who may have had several cultural encounters, also must have a genuine desire and the motivation to work with clients from diverse cultures. A nurse's words and actions must be congruent with his or her true inner feelings. It is important to grasp the concept of caring to understand fully the construct of cultural desire. It has been said that patients don't care how much you know, until they first know how much you care" (Campinha-Bacote, 1999, p. 205). This type of caring comes from the heart and not from the mouth (Campinha-Bacote, 1998a). The challenge to the nurse is to not offer comments that are politically correct (words from the mouth), but to offer comments that reflect true caring (words from the heart).

Conclusion

The proposed conceptual model of cultural competence can provide rehabilitation nurses with guidelines and a framework to address the issue of culturally competent nursing care. The goal of practicing cultural competence is to create a "cultural habit." "Cultural habit is the intersection of awareness, knowledge, skill, encounters, and desire" (Campinha-Bacote, 1998a, p. 49). Along this cultural journey, the nurse must not fear making mistakes. As Rolfe Kerr expresses in his personal creed, "Do not fear mistakes—fear only the absence of creative, constructive, and corrective responses to those mistakes" (Covey, 1989, p. 106). This proposed model can provide rehabilitation nurses with creative, constructive, and correct responses for providing culturally responsive care.

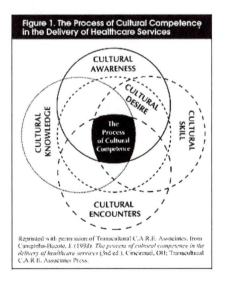

Figure 1

Application of the Model

References

Association of Rehabilitation Nurses. (1996). *Appropriate inclusion of rehabilitation nurses wherever rehabilitation is provided.* Glenview, IL: Author.

Banja, J. (1996). Ethics, values and world culture: The impact on rehabilitation. *Disability and Rehabilitation, 18*, 279–284.

Berlin, E., & Fowkes, W. (1982). A teaching framework for cross-cultural health care. *The Western Journal of Medicine, 139*, 934–938.

Buchwald, D., Caralis, P.V., Gany, F., Hardt, E.T., Johnson, T.M., Muech, M.A., & Putsch, R.W. (1994). Caring for patients in a multicultural society. *Patient Care, 28*(11), 105–123.

Campinha-Bacote, J. (1995). The quest for cultural competence in nursing care. *Nursing Forum, 40*(4), 19–25.

Campinha-Bacote, J. (1998a). *The process of cultural competence in the delivery of healthcare services* (3rd ed.). Cincinnati, OH: Transcultural C.A.R.E. Associates Press.

Campinha-Bacote, J. (1998b). African-Americans. In L. Purnell & B. Paulanka (Eds.), *Transcultural health care: A culturally competent approach* (pp. 53–73). Philadelphia: F.A. Davis.

Campinha-Bacote, J. (1999). A model and instrument to address cultural competence in health care. *Journal of Nursing Education, 38*, 203–207.

Covey, S. (1989). *The seven habits of highly effective people.* New York: Simon & Schuster.

Giger, J., & Davidhizar, R. (1999). *Transcultural nursing.* St. Louis: Mosby Year Book.

Kleinman, A., Eisenburg, L., & Good, B. (1978). Culture, illness, and care. *Annals of Internal Medicine, 88*, 251.

Leininger, M. (1967). The concept of culture and its relevance to nursing. *Journal of Nursing Education, 6*(2), 27.

Leininger, M. (1978). *Transcultural nursing: Concepts, theories, research, and practice.* New York: John Wiley & Sons.

Application of the Model

Leininger, M. (1995). *Transcultural nursing: Concepts, theories, research, and practice* (2nd ed.). New York: McGraw-Hill, Inc.

Meleis, A., & Meleis, M. (1998). Egyptian-Americans. In L. Purnell & B. Paulanka (Eds.), *Transcultural health care: A culturally competent approach* (pp. 217–243). Philadelphia: F.A. Davis.

National Institutes of Health Consensus Development Panel (1998). NIH consensus statements for the rehabilitation of persons with traumatic brain injury. *NIH Consensus Statement, 16*(1), 1–41.

Purnell, L. (2000). A description of the Purnell model for cultural competence. *Journal of Transcultural Nursing, 11*(1), 40–46.

Purnell, L., & Paulanka, B. (1998). *Transcultural health care: A culturally competent approach*. Philadelphia: F.A. Davis.

Reizan, A., & Meleis, A. (1986). Arab-American perceptions of and responses to pain. *Critical Care Nurse, 6*, 30–36.

Sue, D., Bernier, J., Durran, A., Feinburg, L., Pedersen, P., Smith, C., & Vasquez-Nuttall, G. (1982). Cross-cultural counseling competencies. *The Counseling Psychologist, 19*(2), 45–52.

Tervalon, M., & Murray-Garcia, J. (1998). Cultural humility versus cultural competence: A critical distinction in defining physician training outcomes in multicultural education. *Journal of Health Care for the Poor and Underserved, 9*(2), 117–125.

Cultural Competence:
Have I "ASKED" the Right Questions?

"Adding wings to caterpillars does not create butterflies --- it creates awkward and dysfunctional caterpillars. Butterflies are created through transformation..."

Stephanie Marshal

The Process of Cultural Competence in the Delivery of Healthcare Services is one model to address the many faces of diversity. In addressing the many faces of cultural diversity, healthcare professionals must realize that these faces share a common goal - to obtain quality healthcare services that are culturally responsive and culturally relevant to their specific cultural group. In providing these culturally responsive services, I suggest that the healthcare professional consider the following question: "In caring for this client, have I "ASKED" myself the right questions?" The mnemonic "ASKED" represents self-examination questions regarding one's awareness, skill, knowledge, encounters, and desire (Campinha-Bacote, 2002):

A*wareness*: Am I aware of my personal biases and prejudices towards cultural groups different than mine? Does racism exist?

S*kill*: Do I have the skill to conduct a cultural assessment and perform a culturally-based physical assessment in a sensitive manner?

K*nowledge*: Do I have knowledge of the client's worldview and the field of biocultural ecology?

E*ncounters*: How many face-to-face encounters have I had with clients from diverse cultural backgrounds?

D*esire*: Do I really "want to" be culturally competent?

The ASKED model is a subjective, self-assesment of a healthcare professional's level of cultural competence. If healthcare professionals want a formal self-assesment, I suggest they consider taking the Inventory for Assessing the Process of Cultural Competence Among Healthcare Professionals - Revised (IAPCC-R). This instrument is displayed in Appendix D.

Cultural Competence: Have I "ASKED" the Right Questions?

After 10 years of reflection on the development of my model of cultural competence, I clearly see that cultural competence is more than the task of seeking awareness, knowledge, skills and encounters. There is a spiritual component that cannot be overlooked (Campinha-Bacote, in press). The key to cultural competence is found in one's will or desire to engage in the process of becoming culturally competent. I now view cultural desire, not as an additional construct that I added to my model in 1998, but rather a pivotal spiritual concept that provides the energy source and foundation for one's journey towards cultural competence.

A healthcare professionals' journey towards cultural competence will depend on their perception. Here is an example: Create a phrase by unscrambling the letters in the second word below. Write your response on the blank line.

Opportunity ISNOWHERE

Opportunity _____.

How did you fill in the blank? Some of you may have perceived the phrase, "Opportunity IS NO WHERE," when trying to unscramble the letters in ISNOWHERE. This is a common reading, for we assume the words "is" and "no" are natural parts of a phrase. However, let's go beyond what we are accustomed to seeing and consider other possibilities. One such possibility is to see the phrase, "Opportunity IS NOW HERE!" Coming from Massachusetts, I unscrambled the letters ISNOWHERE to read, "I SNOW HERE." When I was conducting a workshop in North Carolina, one healthcare professional saw the possibility, "I'S NOW HERE." All of these creative phrases go beyond what we assume we see in the scrambled letters. In your personal journey towards cultural competence, I challenge you to see beyond the color of a client's skin, physical size, religion, or socio-economic status. When interacting with diverse cultural groups, take the attitude that "Opportunity IS NOW HERE!"

I am still on my personal journey towards cultural competence, for cultural competence is a process, not an event; cyclic, not linear; dynamic, not static; a process of becoming, not being; a journey, not a destination; and coming to terms with the paradox of knowing:

> "The more you think you know; the more you
> really don't know. The more you think you
> don't know; the more you really know."

Bibliography

Allender, B. (1999). <u>The Healing Path</u>. Colorado Springs, CO: WaterBrook Press.

<u>American Nurses Association Position Statement on Discrimination and Racism in Health Care</u>. (2002). Retrieved December 28, 2002.
Available at: <u>http://www.nursingworld.org/readroom/position/ethics/etdisrac.htm</u>

Barbee, E. (2002). Racism and Mental Health. <u>Journal of the American Psychiatric Nurses Association</u>, 8(6), 194-199.

Beer, J. (1998). <u>Racism and Prejudice</u>. Cross-Cultural Communication Course, Spring, 98, Course# 33.140. Week Nine: Culture at Work - Diversity, the "isms." School of International Service, American University, Washington, DC. Retrieved on January 4, 2003. Available at: <u>http://www.culture-at-work.com/xcc.html</u>

Bell, P., and Evans, J. (1981). <u>Counseling the Black Client</u>. Center City, MN: Hazelden Education Materials.

Benner, P. (1984). <u>From Novice to Expert: Excellence and Power in Clinical Nursing Practice</u>. CA: Addison-Wesley Publishing, Co.

Berlin, E., and Fowkes, W. (1982). A Teaching Framework for Cross-Cultural Health Care. <u>The Western Journal of Medicine</u>, 139(6), 934-938.

Bloch, B. (1983). Bloch's Assessment Guide for Ethnic/ Cultural Variations. In M. Orque, B. Bloch & L. Monroy (Eds.), <u>Ethnic Nursing Care</u>. St. Louis: C.V. Mosby Co.

Borkan, J., and Neher, J. (1991). A Developmental Model of Ethnicity in Family Practice Training. <u>Family Medicine</u>, 23(3), 212.

Bibliography

Buchwald, D., Caralis, P., Gany, F., Hardt, E., Johnson, T., Mueche, M., and Putsh, R. (1994). Caring for Patients in a Multicultural Society. Patient Care, 28(11), 105-123.

Campinha-Bacote, J. (2003). Many Faces: Addressing Diversity in Health Care. Journal of Online Issues in Nursing, 8(1). At: http://nursingworld.org/ojin/topic20/tpc20_2.htm

Campinha-Bacote, J. (in press). Cultural Desire: The Development of a Spiritual Construct of Cultural Competence. Journal of Christian Nursing (Summer 2003).

Campinha-Bacote, J. (2002). Cultural Competence in Psychiatric Nursing: Have you ASKED the Right Questions? Journal of the American Psychiatric Nurses Association, 8(6), 183-187.

Campinha-Bacote, J. and Narayan, M. (2000). Culturally Competent Health Care in the Home. Home Care Provider, 5(6) 213-219.

Campinha-Bacote, J., and Campinha-Bacote, D. (1999). A Framework for Providing Culturally Competent Health Care Services in Managed Care Organizations. Journal of Transcultural Nursing, 10(3), 291-292.

Campinha-Bacote, J. (1999). A Model and Instrument for Addressing Cultural Competence in Health Care. Journal of Nursing Education, 38(5), 203-207.

Campinha-Bacote, J. (1998). The Process of Cultural Competence in the Delivery Healthcare Services: A Culturally Competent Model of Care (3rd Edition). Cincinnati, OH: Transcultural C.A.R.E. Associates.

Campinha-Bacote, J. (1997). Cultural Competence: A Critical Factor in Child Health Policy. Journal of Pediatric Nursing, 12(4), 260-262.

Campinha-Bacote, J. (1996). A Culturally Competent Model of Nursing Management. Surgical Services Management, 2(5), 22-25.

Campinha-Bacote, J., Yahle, T. and Langerkamp, M. (1996). The Challenge of Cultural Diversity for Nurse Educators. Journal of Continuing Education in Nursing, 27(2), 59-64.

Bibliography

Campinha-Bacote, J. and Padgett, J. (1995). Cultural Competence: A Critical Factor in Nursing Research. Journal of Cultural Diversity, 2(1), 31-34.

Campinha-Bacote, J. (1995). Transcultural Psychiatric Nursing: Diagnostic and Treatment Issues. Journal of Psychosocial Nursing, 32(8), 41-46.

Campinha-Bacote, J. (1991). Community Mental Health Services for the Underserved: A Culturally Specific Model. Archives of Psychiatric Nursing, 5(4), 229-235.

Campinha-Bacote, J., and Ferguson, S. (1991). Cultural Considerations in Child Rearing Practices: A Transcultural Perspective. Journal of National Black Nurses' Association, 5(1), 11-17.

Carillo, J., Green, A., and Betancourt, J. (1999). Cross-cultural Primary Care: A Patient-based Approach. Annals of Internal Medicine, 130, 829-834.

Clarke, W., Hewson, M. and Fry, M. (1996). Three Function Card. Available at: http://www.physicianpatient.org/products.html#publications

Cross, T., Bazron, B., Dennis, K., and Isaac, M. (1989). Toward a Culturally Competent System of Care. PA: CASSP Technical Assistance Center at Georgetown University Child Development Center.

Culhane-Pera, K. (1996). The Cultural Competence Continuum. Cited in The Center for Cross-Cultural Health. (1997). Caring Across Cultures: The Provider's Guide to Cross-Cultural Health Care, MN: Author.

DelBello, M., Soutuillo, C., Ochsner, J., et. al. (1999). Racial Differences in the Treatment of Adolescents With Bipolar Disorder. New Research 379. Presented at the 152nd Annual Meeting of the American Psychiatric Association, May 18th in Washington, DC.

Diagnostic and Statistical Manual of Mental Disorders: DSM-IV. (1994). Washington, DC: American Psychiatric Association.

Bibliography

Eisenberg, D., Davis, R., Etter, L., et al. (1998). Trends in Alternative Medicine use in the United States, 1990-1997: Results of a Follow-up National Survey. JAMA, 280, 1569-1575.

Eisenberg, D., Kessler, R., Foster, D. et al. (1993). Unconventional Medicine in the United States: Prevalence, Costs and Patterns of Use. New England Journal of Medicine, 328, 246-252.

Fong, C. (1985). Ethnicity and Nursing Practice. Topics in Clinical Nursing, 7(3), 1-10.

Dreyfus, H., and Dreyfus, S. (1980). A Five-Stage Model of the Mental Activities Involved in Directed Skill Acquisition. Operations Research Center Report, February, 1980.

Dube', C., Goldman, R., and Monroe, A. (1998). Introduction to Culture and Medical Interactions. In C. Dube', R. Rosen, J. Toohey, et al (Eds.), Communication Skills for Breast and Cervical Cancer Screening: A Curriculum for Medical Students: Module Three. Providence, RI: Brown University.

Galanti, G. (1991). Caring for Patients From Different Cultures. PA: University of Pennsylvania Press.

Harwood, A. (1981). Ethnicity and Medical Care. MA: Harvard University Press.

Giger, J., and Davidhizar, R. (1999). Transcultural Nursing. St. Louis: Mosby Year Book.

Jacobsen, F. (1988). Ethnocultural Assessment. In L. Comaz-Diaz (Eds.), Clinical Guidelines in Cross-Cultural Mental Health.

Kaufert, J., and Putsch, R. (1997). Communication Through Interpreters in Healthcare: Ethical Dilemmas Arising From Differences in Class, Culture, Language, and Power. Journal of Clinical Ethics, 8(1), 71-87.

Kleinman, A. Eisenburg, L.M. and Good, B. (1978). Culture, Illness and Care. Annals of Internal Medicine, 88, 251.

Bibliography

Kleinman, A. (1980). <u>Patients and Healers in the Context of Culture</u>. CA: University of California Press.

Koempel, V. (2003). <u>Cultural Competence of Certified Nurse Practitioners</u>. Masters Thesis. Minnesota State University, Mankato, MN.

Lara, G. (1997). <u>Strategies to Improve Health Status for Women of Color</u>. Paper presented at the Women of Color Health Conference: Collaborating Today for a Healthy Tomorrow. This conference was held in June 1997 at Michigan State University, College of Human Medicine in East Lansing, Michigan.

Lavizzo-Mourey, R. (1996). Cultural Competence: Essential Measurements of Quality for Managed Care Organizations. <u>Annals of Internal Medicine</u>, 124(10), 919-921.

Law, E. (1993). <u>The Wolf Shall Dwell With The Lamb</u>. St. Louis, Missouri: Chalice Press.

Lawson, W. (1999). <u>Ethnicity and Treatment of Bipolar Disorder</u>. Presented at the 152nd Annual Meeting of the American Psychiatric Association on May 19th in Washington, DC.

Leff, J. (1981). <u>Psychiatry Around the Globe</u>. NY: Marcel Dekker, Inc.

Leininger, M. (1995). <u>Transcultural Nursing: Theories, Concepts and Practices</u>, (2nd Ed.) NY: McGraw Hill, Inc.

Leininger, M. (1978). <u>Transcultural Nursing: Theories, Concepts and Practices</u>. NY: John Wiley & Sons.

Leininger, M. (1967). The Culture Concept and its Relevance to Nursing. <u>Journal of Nursing Education</u>, 6(2), 27.

Levy, R. (1993). <u>Ethnic and Racial Differences in Response to Medication</u>. VA: National Pharmaceutical Council.

Bibliography

Levin, S., Like, R., and Gottlieb, J. (2000). ETHNIC: A Framework for Culturally Competent Clinical Practice. New Brunswick, NJ: Department of Family Medicine, UMDNJ-Robert Wood Johnson Medical School.

Like, R. (2000). TRANSLATE: For Working With Medical Interpreters. Patient Care, 34(9), 188.

Lin, K., Poland, R., and Lesser, I. (1986). Ethnicity and Psychopharmacology. Culture, Medicine, and Psychiatry, 10, 151-165.

McGoldrick, M. (1982). Normal Families: An Ethnic Perspective. In F. Walsh (Ed.), Normal Family Process. NY: Guilford Press.

MacIntosh, P. (1989). White Privilege: Unpacking the Invisible Knapsack. Peace and Freedom, July/August, 10-12.

McNeil, J., Campinha-Bacote, J., and Vample, G. (2002). BESAFE: National Minority AIDS Education and Training Center Cultural Competency Model. Washington, DC: Howard Medical School.

Nichols, E. (1987). Nichols' Model of the Philosophical Aspects of Cultural Difference. Unpublished paper. Contact: Nichols and Associates, Inc.; 1523 Underwood Street, NW; Washington, DC, 20012.

Parreno, H. (1977). Cultural Health Traditions: Implications for Nursing Care - Oriental Culture. Cited in Orque, M., Bloch, B., and Monroy, L. (1983), Ethnic Nursing Care. St. Louis: C.V. Mosby Co.

Pedersen, P. (1988). A Handbook for Multicultural Awareness. VA: American Association for Counseling and Development.

Purnell, L. (1998). Transcultural Diversity and Health Care. In L. Purnell and B. Paulanka (Eds.), Transcultural Health Care: A Culturally Competent Approach. PA: F.A. Davis.

Purnell, L. and Paulanka, B. (1998). Transcultural Health Care: A Culturally Competent Approach. PA: F.A. Davis.

Bibliography

Recommendations From the Minnesota Public Health Association's Immigrant Health Task Force. (1996). Six Steps Towards Cultural Competence. MN: Author.

Rogers, C. (1951). Client-centered Therapy. MA: Houghton Mifflin.

Satel. (2000). PC, MD: How Political Correctness is Corrupting Medicine. Washington, DC: AEI Press.

Schaeffeler, E., Eichelbaum, M., Brinkmann, U., Penger, A., Asante-Poku, S., Zanger, U., and Schwab, M. (2001). Frequency of C3435T Polymorphism of MDR1 Gene in African People. Lancet, 358, 383-384.

Smedley, B., Stith, A., and Nelson, A. (2002). Unequal Treatment: Confronting Racial and Ethnic Disparities in Health Care. Board on Health Sciences Policy. Institute of Medicine. Washington, DC: National Academic Press.

Strakowski, S., McElroy, S., Keck, P., and West, S. (1996). Racial Influence on Diagnosis in Psychotic Mania. Journal of Affective Disorders, 39(2), 157-162.

Strickland, T., Lin, K., Fu, P., et al. (1995). Comparison of Lithium Ratio Between African-American and Caucasian Bipolar Patients. Biological Psychiatry, 37(5), 325-330.

Stuart, M., and Lieberman, J. (1993). The Fifteen Minute Hour: Applied Psychotherapy for the Primary Care Physician (2nd ed.). New York, NY: Praeger.

Sue, D., Bernier, J., Durran, A., Feinburg, L., Pedersen, P., Smith, C., and Vasquez-Nuttall, G. (1982). Cross-Cultural Counseling Competencies. The Counseling Psychologist, 19(2), 45-52.

Schwartz, R. (2001). Racial Profiling in Medical Research. New England Journal of Medicine, 433, 1392-1393.

Takeshita , T., Yang, X., Inoue, Y, et al. (2000). Relationship Between Alcohol Drinking, ADH2 and ALDH2 Genotypes, and Risk for Hepatocellar Carcinoma in Japanese. Cancer Letter, 149(1-2), 69-76.

Bibliography

Tervalon, M., and Murray-Garcia, J. (1998). Cultural Humility versus cultural Competence: A Critical Distinction in Defining Physician Training Outcomes in Multicultural Education {editorial}. <u>Journal of Health Care for the Poor and Underserved</u>, 9(2), 117-125.

Tylor, 2. (1871). <u>Primitive Culture</u>. Volume 1. London: Bradbury, Evans and Co.

U.S. Department of Health and Human Services. (2001). <u>Mental Health: Culture, Race, and Ethnicity - A Supplement to Mental Health: A Report of the Surgeon General</u>. Rockville, MD: U.S. Department of Health and Human Services, Substance Abuse and Mental Health Services Administration, Center for Mental Health Services, National Institutes of Health, National Institute of Mental Health.

Wenger, F. (1998). Cultural Openness, Social Justice, Global Awareness: Promoting Transcultural Nursing With Unity in a Diverse World. In P. Merilainen & K. Vehvilainen-Julkunen (Eds.), <u>The 23rd Annual Nursing Research Conference 1997</u>: <u>Transcultural Nursing - Global Unifier of Care Facing Diversity With Unity</u> (pp. 162-168). Kuopio, Finland: Kuopio University Publications.

Appendix A

National Standards for Culturally

and Linguistically Appropriate

Services (CLAS) in Health Care

CLAS

1. Health care organizations should ensure that patients/consumers receive from all staff members effective understandable, and respectful care that is provided in a manner compatible with their cultural health belief and practices and preferred language.

2. Health care organizations should implement strategies to recruit, retain, and promote at all levels of the organization a diverse staff and leadership that are representative of the demographic characteristic of the service area.

3. Health care organizations should ensure that staff at all levels and across disciplines receive ongoing education and training in culturally and linguistically appropriate service delivery.

4. Health care organizations must offer and provide language assistance services, including bilingual staff and interpreter services, at no cost to each patient/consumer with Limited English proficiency at all points of contact, in a timely manner during all hours of operation.

5. Health care organizations must provide to patients/consumers in their preferred language both verbal and written notices informing them of their rights to receive language assistance services.

6. Health care organizations must assure the competence of language assistance provided to limited English proficient patients/consumers by interpreters and bilingual staff. Family and friends should not be used to provide interpretation services (except on request by the patient/consumer).

7. Health care organizations must make available easily understood patient-related materials and post signage in the languages of the commonly encountered groups and/or groups represented in the service area.

8. Health care organizations should develop, implement, and promote written strategic plans, and management account-ability/oversight mechanisms to provide culturally and linguistically appropriate services.

9. Health care organizations should conduct initial and ongoing organizational self-assessments of CLAS-related activities and are encouraged to integrate cultural and linguistic competence-related measures into their internal audits, performance improvement plans, patient satisfaction assessments, and outcomes-based evaluations.

10. Health care organizations should ensure that data on the individual patient's/consumer's race, ethnicity, and spoken and written language are collected in health records, integrated into the organization's management information systems, and periodically updated.

11. Health care organizations should maintain a current demographic, cultural, and epidemiological profile of the community as well as a needs assessment to accurately plan for and implement services that respond to the cultural and linguistic characteristics of the service area.

12. Health care organizations should develop participatory, collaborative partnerships with communities and utilize a variety of informal and formal mechanisms to facilitate community and patient/consumer involvement in designing and implementing CLAS-related activities.

13. Health care organizations should ensure that conflict and grievance resolution processes are culturally and linguistically sensitive and capable of identifying, preventing, and resolving cross-cultural conflicts or complaints by patients/consumers.

14. Health care organizations are encouraged to regularly make available to the public information about their progress and successful innovations in implementing the CLAS standards and to provide public notice in their communities about the availability of this information.

Appendix B

References &Website Links

References

Barnett, B. (1999). Clinical and Cultural Issues in Caring for Deaf People. Family Medicine, 31 (10), 17-22.

Brach, C. & Fraser, I. (2000). Can Cultural Competency Reduce Racial and Ethnic Health Disparities? A Review and Conceptual Model. Managed Care Research and Review, 57 (Suppl. 1) 181-217.

Burroughs, V., Maxey, R., & Levy, R. (2002). Racial and Ethnic Differences in Response to Medicines: Towards Individualized Treatment. Journal of the National Medical Association, 94:1-26.

Byrd, W.M., Clayton, LA, (2002). An American Health Dilemma. Volume 2- Race, Medicine and Health Care in the United States 1900-2000. NY: Routledge.

Campinha-Bacote, J. (2003). Many Faces: Addressing Diversity in Health Care. Journal of Online Issues in Nursing, 8(1). At: http://nursingworld.org/ojin/topic20/tpc20_2.htm

Campinha-Bacote, J. (2002). The Process of Cultural Competence in the Delivery of Healthcare Services: A Model of Care. Journal of Transcultural Nursing, 13 (3), 181-184.

Campinha-Bacote, J. (2002). Readings and Resources in Transcultural Health Care and Mental Health (13th Edition). OH: Transcultural C.A.R.E. Associates Press (order address: Transcultural C.A.R.E. Associates; 11108 Huntwicke Place; Cincinnati, Ohio 45241 or call: 1-513-469-1664; E-Mail: meddir@aol.com).

Campinha-Bacote, J. (1999). A Model and Instrument for Addressing Cultural Competence in Health Care. Journal of Nursing Education, 38(5), 203-207.

Campinha-Bacote, J., and Munoz, C. (2001). A Guiding Framework for Delivering Culturally Competent Services in Case Management. The Case Manager, 12(2), 48-52.

References

Campinha-Bacote, J. (1998). The Process of Cultural Competence in the Delivery of Healthcare Services (3rd Edition). OH: Transcultural C.A.R.E. Associates Press (order address: Transcultural C.A.R.E. Associates; 11108 Huntwicke Place; Cincinnati, Ohio 45241 or call 1-513-469-1664. E-Mail: meddir@aol.com).

Carillo, J.E., Green, A.R., & Betancourt, J.R. (1999). Cross-Cultural Primary Care; A Patient-based Approach. Annals of Internal Medicine, 130:829-834.

Chin, J.L. (2000). Culturally Competent Health Care. Public Reports, 11(5), 25-33.

Chong, N. (2002). The Latino Patient: A Cultural Guide for Health Care Providers. ME: Intercultural Press.

Clark, C., and Robinson, T.M. (1999). Cultural Diversity and Transcultural Nursing as They Impact Health Care. Journal of National Black Nurses' Association, 10(2), 46-53.

Dean, Ruth. (2001). The Myth of Cross-Cultural Competence. Families in Society, 82(6), 623-630.

Epstein, A. & Ayanian, J. (2001). Racial Disparities in Medical Care. New England Journal of Medicine, 344:1471-73.

Fadiman, A. (1997). The Spirit Catches You and You Fall Down. NY: Farrar, Straus and Giroux.

Fiscella, K., Franks, P., Gold, MR., & Clancy, CM. (2000). Inequality in Quality: Addressing Socioeconomic, Racial, and Ethnic Disparities in Health Care. JAMA, 283:2579-84.

Flores, G. (2000). Culture and the Patient-Physician Relationship: Achieving Cultural Competency in Health Care. The Journal of Pediatrics, 136, 14-23.

References

Fortier, J., Convissor, R. & Pacheco, G. (1999). <u>Assuring Cultural Competence in Health Care: Recommendations for National Standards and Outcomes-Focused Research Agenda</u>. Produced for U.S. Department of health and Human Service Office of Minority Health under contracts #97T2261501D and #97T27190901D.

Giger, J., & Davidhizar, R. (1999). <u>Transcultural Nursing</u>. St. Louis: Mosby Year Book.

Geiger, H.J. (2001). Racial Stereotyping and Medicine: The Need for Cultural Competence. <u>Canadian Medical Association Journal</u>, 164 (2), 1699-1701.

Grypma, S., & Taylor, S. (1999). Packing for the Journey: Character Traits for Transcultural Care. <u>Journal of Christian Nursing</u>, 16(4), 13-16.

Helman, C. (2000). <u>Culture, Health and Illness</u> (4th Ed.). MA: Butterworth-Heineman.

Institute on Health Care for the Poor and Underserved. (1998). Papers Published from the "Forum on Language Barriers to Care." <u>Journal of Health Care for the Poor and Underserved</u>, Vol. 9; Supplemental, S5-S95.

Jones, C.P. (2000). Levels of Racism: A Theoretic Framework and a Gardener's Tale. <u>American Journal of Public Health</u>, 90(8), 1212-1215.

Kagawa-Singer, M., & Blackhall, L.J. (2001). Negotiating Cross-Cultural Issues at the End of Life. <u>JAMA</u>, 286:2993-3001.

Kavanagh, K., Absolam, K., Beil, W., & Schliessmann, L. (1999). Connecting and Becoming Culturally Competent: A Lakota Example. <u>Advanced Nursing Science</u>, 21(3), 9-31.

Henry J. Kaiser Family Foundation. (1999). <u>Key Facts: Race, Ethnicity & Medical Care</u>. Menlo Park, CA: Author.

Huff, R.M., & Kline, M.V. (1999). <u>Promoting Health in Multicultural Populations: A Handbook for Practitioners</u>. Thousand Oaks, CA: Sage.

References

Journal of Transcultural Nursing. (2002). Entire July issue (Volume 13, Issue 3) focuses on the extant models, theories & frameworks of transcultural nursing.

Kudzma, EC. (1999). Culturally Competent Drug Administration. American Journal of Nursing, 99(8), 46-51.

Leigh, J.W. (1998). Communication for Culture Competence. Boston, MA: Allyn & Bacon.

Leuning, D., Swiggum, P., Wiegert, H., & McCullough-Zander. (2002). Proposed Standards for Transcultural Nursing. Journal of Transcultural Nursing, 13(1), 40-46.

Lipson, J. (1996). Culture and Nursing Care: a Pocket Guide. CA: University of San Francisco Nursing Press.

Maclean, JR., Johnson, M., Rogers, R.L., & Hoffman, W. (2002). Collecting Data on Race and Ethnicity in Managed Care: Challenges and Suggestions. JCOM, 9(5), 259-262.

McNeil, J., Campinha-Bacote, J., & Vample, G. (2002). BESAFE: National Minority AIDS Education and Training Center Cultural Competency Model. Washington, DC: Howard University Medical School. http://www.nmaetc.org/cultural/cultural.asp

Misener, T.R., Sowell, R.L., Phillips, K.D., & Harris, C. (1997). Sexual Orientation: A Cultural Diversity Issue for Nursing. Nursing Outlook, 45(4), 178-181.

Papadopoulous, I., & Lee, S. (2002). Developing Culturally Competent Researchers. Journal of Advanced Nursing, 37(3), 258-264.

Patient Care. (2000). "Caring for Diverse Populations: Breaking Down Barriers." The entire journal of Patient Care, May 15, 2000, Volume 34, Issue 9, is focused on healthcare delivery in diverse populations.

References

Polaschek, N.R. (1998). Cultural Safety: A New Concept in Nursing People of Different Ethnicities. Journal of Advanced Nursing, 27(3), 452-457.

Pollock, S.E. (1999). Health-related Hardiness With Different Ethnic Populations. Nursing Practice, 13(3), 1-10.

Purnell, L. (2000). A Description of the Purnell Model for Cultural Competence. Journal of Transcultural Nursing, 11(1), 40-46.

Purnell, L., & Paulanka, B. (1998). Transcultural Health Care: A Culturally Competent Approach. PA: F.A. Davis.

Rassool, G.H. (2000). The Crescent and Islam: Healing, Nursing and the Spiritual Dimension. Some Considerations Towards and Understanding of the Islamic Perspectives on Caring. Journal of Advanced Nursing, 32(6), 1476-1484.

Remus, B., & Handler. (2001). Cultural Competence is a Must for all Hospitals. Hospital Case Management. February, 22-30.

Richardson, L.D. (1999). Patient's Rights and Professional Responsibilities: The Moral Case for Cultural Competence. Mount Sinai Journal of Medicine, 66(4), 267-270.

Salimbene, S. (2000). What Language Does Your Patient Hurt In? Amherst, MA: Diversity Resources Publishers.

Smedley, B.D., Stith, A.Y., & Nelson, A.R. (2002). Unequal Treatment: Confronting Racial and Ethnic Disparities in Health Care. Board on Health Sciences Policy. Institute of Medicine. Washington, DC: National Academic Press.

Smith, LS. (1998). Concept Analysis: Cultural Competence. Journal of Cultural Diversity, 5(1), 4-10.

Spector, R. (2000). Cultural Diversity in Health and Illness. CT: Appleton-Lange.

References

Tervalon, M., & Murray-Garcia, J. (1998). Cultural Humility versus Cultural Competence: A Critical Distinction in Defining Physician Training Outcomes in Multicultural Education {editorial}. Journal of Health Care for the Poor and Underserved, 9(2), 117-125.

Wells, SA. & Black, R.M. (2000). Cultural Competency for Health Professionals. Bethesda, MD: American Occupational Therapy Association, Inc.

Wells, M.I. (2000). Beyond Cultural Competence: A Model for Individual and Institutional Development. Journal of Community Health Nursing, 17(4), 189-199.

Website Links

-   **The Provider 's Guide to Quality and Culture**

    http://erc.msh.org/quality&culture

-   **Culturally &Linguistically Appropriate Services**

    www.omhrc.gov/clas

-   **Center for Healthy Families and Culture Diversity**

    http://www2.umdnj.edu/fmedweb/chfcd/INDEX.HTM

-   **Ethnomed**

    http://ethnomed.org/

-   **Compendium of Cultural Competence Initiatives in Health Care**

    http://www.kff.org/content/2003/6067

-   **Initiative to Eliminate Racial and Ethnic Disparities in Health**

    http://raceandhealth.hhs.gov

-   **CulturedMed**

    http://www.sunyit.edu/library/html/culturedmed/

-   **National Center For Cultural Competence**

    http://www.georgetown.edu/research/gucdc/nccc/

-   **Cross Cultural Health Care**

    http://www.xculture.org/

-   **National Multicultural Institute**

    http://www.nmci.org

Website Links

- **Diversity in Medicine**

  http://www.amsa.org/div/

- **Resources for Cross-Cultural Health Care**

  http://www.diversityrx.org/

- **Transcultural &Multicultural Health Links**

  http://www.iun.edu/~libemb/trannurs/trannurs.htm

- **The Center for Cross-Cultural Health**

  http://www.crosshealth.com/

- **Multilingual Glossary of Medical Terms**

  http://allserv.rug.ac.be/~rvdstich/eugloss/welcome.html

- **Cultural Medicine**

  http://www.geocities.com/SoHo/Study/8276/CulturalMed.html

- **Transcultural Nursing Society**

  http://www.tcns.org

Incorporating Cultural Concepts into the Health Professions' Curriculum

Abrums, M.E.,& Leppa, C. (2000). Beyond Cultural Competence: Teaching About Race, Gender, Class and Sexual Orientation. Journal of Nursing Education, 40(6), 270-275.

Adams, J.Q., & Welsch. (1999). Cultural Diversity: Curriculum, Classroom and Climate. Western Illinois University Foundation.

American Institutes For Research. (2002). Teaching Cultural Competence in Health Care: A Review of Current Concepts, Policies and Practices. Washington, DC: Office of Minority Health, U.S. Department of Health and Human Services. Contract Number: 282-98-0029; Task Order #41; Task 2: Synthesis Report, March 12,2002.

American Academy of Pediatrics. (1998). Culturally Effective Pediatric Care: Education and Training Issues. Pediatrics, 103(1), 167-170.

Association of American Medical Colleges. (1998). Teaching and Learning of Cultural Competence in Medical School. Contemporary Issues in Medical Education, 1(5).

Asian Voice: Asian and Asian-American Health Educators Speak Out. (1997). NY: NLN Press.

Bailey, D. (2000). Introducing Awareness of Cultural Diversity into an Established Curriculum. In, P.A. Crist (Ed. Beth.), Innovations in Occupational Therapy Education. Bethesda, MD: American Occupational Therapy Association, Inc.

Baker, C. (1997). Cultural Relativity and Cultural Diversity: Implications for Nursing Practice. Advances in Nursing Science, 20(1), 3-11.

Banks, J.A., &Banks, CM. (1997). Multicultural Education: Issues and Perspectives. MA: Allyn &Bacon.

Barbee, E., &Gibson, S. (2001). Our Dismal Progress: The Recruitment of Non-Whites into Nursing. Journal of Nursing Education,40(6), 243-244.

Black, R.M. (2001). Comparison of Multicultural Literature in Three Health Professions: Physical Therapy, Nursing and Social Work. Journal of Nursing Education, 41:117-120.

References

Blackford, J. (1997). Cultural Frameworks of Nursing Practice: Situating the Self. Nursing Inquiry, 4,205-207.

Brainin-Rodriquez, J.E. (2001). A Course About Culture and Gender in the Clinical Setting for Third Year Students. Academic Medicine, 76, 512-513.

Campinha-Bacote, J. (2002). Readings &Resources in Transcultural Health Care &Mental Health (13th Edition). Cincinnati, OH: Transcultural C.A.R.E. Associates: 11108 Huntwicke Place, Cincinnati, OH 45241 (1-513-469-1664; meddir@aol.com).

Campinha-Bacote, J. (1998). Cultural Diversity in Nursing Education: Issues and Concerns. Journal of Nursing Education, 37(1), 3-4.

Canales, M., Bowers, B.J., & Norton, S.A. (2000). Becoming Part of a Community: Teaching Strategies of Latina Nursing Faculty. Nursing &Health Care Perspectives, 21(5), 228-233.

Carillo, J.E., Green, A.R., & Betancourt, J.R. (c.a. 1999). Cross-Cultural Primary Care: A Patient-Based Approach. An 8 hour curriculum for medical students and residents using lectures, video-taped patient vignettes and practice interviews with patient surrogates. Contact Dr. Betancourt at the Center for Multicultural and Minority Health: NY Presbyterian Hospital-Cornell Internal Medicine Associates; 505 East 70th Street-HT4, NY, NY 10021 or call 1-212-746-2958.

Chrisman, N., & Schultz. (1998). Transforming Healthcare through Cultural Competence Training. In J. Dieneman (Ed.), Cultural Diversity in Nursing: Issues, Strategies and Outcomes, Washington, D.C.: American Academy of Nursing.

Chrisman, N.J. (1998 Jan.). Faculty Infrastructure for Cultural Competence. Journal of Nursing Education, 37 (1), 45-47.

Clark, L. & Thornam, C. (2002). Using Educational Technology to Teach Cultural Assessment. Journal of Nursing Education, 412: 117-120.

Clark, L., Zuk, J., & Barame, J. (2000). A Literacy Approach to Teaching Cultural Competence. Journal of Transcultural Nursing, 11(3), 199-202.

Culhane-Pera, K., Like, R., Lebensohn-Chialvo, P., & Loewe, R. (2000). Multicultural Curricula in Family Practice Residence. Family Medicine, 32(2), 167-173.

References

Dreachslin, J., Jacobs, E., Putsch, R., Weech -Maldonado, R., &Welch, M. (2002). Concept Papers Commissioned for the Development of Culturally Competent Curricula Modules. Washington, D.C.: Office of Minority Health, U.S. Department of Health and Human Services and the American Institutes for Research.

Donini-Lenhoff, E.G., &Hendrick, H.L. (2001). Increasing Awareness and Implementation of Cultural Competence Principles in Health Professions Education. Journal of Allied Health, 29(40), 241-245.

Drevdahl, D. (2001). Teaching About Race, Racism and Health. Journal of Nursing Education, 40(6), 270-275.

Fadiman, A. (1997). The Spirit Catches You and You Fall Down. NY: Farrar, Straus and Giroux (the following link provides a teaching guide for facilitating discussion on the topic of cultural conflicts: http://www.fsbassociates.com/fsg/spiritrg.html).

Fahrenwald, N., Boysen, R., & Maurer, R. (2001). Developing Cultural Competence in the Baccalaureate Nursing Student: A Population-Based Project with the Hutterites. Journal of Transcultural Nursing, 12 (1), 48-55.

Ferguson, V. (1999). Case Studies in Cultural Diversity: A Workbook. NY: NLN.

Flavin, C. (1997), Cross-Cultural Training for Nurses: A Research-Based Education Project. The American Journal of Hospice & Palliative Care, 121-126. (May/June issue).

Flores, G., Gee, D., & Kastner, B. (2000). The Teaching of Cultural Issues in U.S. and Canadian Medical Schools. Academic Medicine, 75(5), 451-455.

Gallos, J., Ramsey & Associates. (1997). Teaching Diversity: Listening to the Soul, Speaking From the Heart. CA: Jossey-Bass.

Gannon, M.J., & June, M.L. (1997). Effects of Alternative Instructional Approaches in Cross-Cultural Training Outcomes. International Journal of Intercultural Relations, 21: 429-446.

Gardenswartz, L., & Rowe, A. (1999). Managing Diversity in Health Care Manual: Proven Tools and Activities for leaders and Trainers.

References

Garaz-Trevino, E.S., P., & Venegas-Samuels, K. (1997). A Psychiatric Curriculum Directed to the Care of the Hispanic Patient. Academic Psychiatry, 21(1),1-10.

Gary, F., Sigby, L., & Campbell, D. (1998). Preparing for the 21st Century: Diversity in Nursing Education, Research and Practice. Journal of Professional Nursing, 14, 272-279.

Gerrish, K. (1998). Preparing Nurses to Care for Minority Ethnic Communities. International Nursing Review, 45 (4), 115-116, 118, 127

Giger, J., & Davidhizar, R. (2001). Teaching Culture Within the Nursing Curriculum Using the Giger-Davidhizar Model of Transcultural Nursing Assessment. Journal of Nursing Education, 40(6), 270-275.

Glanville, C., & Porche, D. (2000). Graduate Nursing Faculty: Ensuring Cultural and Racial Diversity Through Faulty Development. Journal of Multicultural Nursing & Health, 6(1), 6-13.

Goldman, R.E., Monroe, A.D., & Dube, C.E. (2001). The Effect of a Global Multiculturalism Track on Cultural Competence of Preclinical Medical Students. Family Medicine, 75(5), 451-455.

Hadwiger, S.C. (1999). Cultural Competence Case Scenarios for Critical Care Nursing Education. Nurse Educator, 24(5), 47-51

Haloburdo, E., & Thompson, M. (1998). A Comparison of International Learning Experiences for Baccalaureate Nursing Students: Developed and Developing Countries. Journal of Nursing Education, 37 (1), 45-47.

Holt, J., Barrett, C., Clarke, D., & Monks, R. (2000). Globalization of Nursing Knowledge. Nurse Education Today, 20, 426-431.

Huff, R.M., &Kline, M.V. (1998). Promoting Health in Multicultural Populations: A Handbook for Practitioners. Thousand Oaks, CA: Sage.

Jeffreys, M.R. (1999). Construct Validation of the Transcultural Self-Efficacy Tool. Journal of Nursing Education, 40(6), 270-275.

Johnson, R. (1997). Mainstreaming Cultural Competency into the Nursing Core Curriculum at the Undergraduate Level. In, Caring for the Emerging Majority: A Blueprint for Action. Health Resources Service Administration, Bureau of Health Professions, Division of Nursing (Ed). Nurse Leadership '97 Invitational Conference Proceedings. Denver, Colorado.

References

Journal of Nursing Education. (1998). Volume 37, Issue 1. This January issue highlights cultural diversity in nursing education.

Journal of the American Medical Women 's Association. (1998). Cultural Competence and Women 's Health in Medical Education. Supplement 1998, Volume 53, Number 3.

Journal of Transcultural Nursing. (2002). Volume 37, Issue 3, presents several theoretical and conceptual models as well as frameworks to organize knowledge about transcultural nursing and health care.

Kai, J., Spencer, J., & Woodward, N. (2001). Wrestling with Ethnic Diversity: Toward Empowering Health Educators. Medical Education, 40(6), 270-275.

Kearns, R.A. (1997). A Place for Cultural Safety Beyond Nursing Education. New Zealand Medical Journal, 110, 23-24.

Killion, C. (2001). Understanding Cultural Aspects of Health Through Photography. Nursing Outlook, 49(1), 50-54.

Kirkpatrick, M.K., Brown, S.E., & Atkins, T.B. (1998). Efficacy of an International Exchange Via Internet. Journal of Nursing Education, 38 (6), 278-281.

Leininger, M. (1998). Nursing Education Exchanges: Concerns and Benefits. Journal of Nursing Education, 9(2), 57-63.

Leininger, M. (1997). Transcultural Nursing Research to Transform Nursing Education and Practice. Image Journal of Nursing Scholarship.

Levine, M.A., (1997). Exploring Cultural Diversity. Journal of Cultural Diversity, 4(2), 53-56.

Li, B., Caniano, D.A., & Comer, R.C. (1998). A Cultural Diversity Curriculum: Combining Didactic, Problem-Solving and Simulated Experience. Journal of the American Medical Women 's Association, 53(3), 128-130.

Like, R., Steiner, P., & Rubel, A. (1996). Recommended Core Curriculum Guidelines on Culturally Sensitive and Competent Health Care. Family Medicine, 75(5), 451-455.

References

Lockhart, J.S., & Resick, L.K. (1997). Teaching Cultural Competence: The Value of Experiential Learning and Community Resources. Nurse Educator, 22(3),27-31.

Loudon, R.F., Anderson, P.M., Gills, P.S., & Greenfield, S.M. (2000). Educating Medical Students for Work in Cultural Diverse Societies. Journal of the American Medical Association, 282(9), 875-880.

Lynch, F.W., &Hanson, M.J. (1998). Developing Cross-Cultural Competence: A Guide for Working with Children and Their Families. Baltimore: Paul H. Brookes.

McCarty, L., Enslein, J., Kelly, L., Choi, E., & Tripp-Reimer, T. (2000). Cross Cultural Health Education: Materials on the World Wide Web. Journal of Transcultural Nursing, 13(1), 54-60.

McGrath, B. (1998). Illness as a Problem: Moving Culture From the Classroom to the Clinic. Advances in Nursing Science, 21, 17-29.

Mock, S.D., Long, G.L., Jones, J.W. Shadick, K., & Solheim, K. (1999). Faculty and Student Cross-Cultural Learning Through Teaching Health Promotion in the Community. Journal of Nursing Education, 40(6), 270-275.

Morey, A., & Kitano, M. (1997). Multicultural Course Transformation in Higher Education: A Broader Truth. Boston, MA: Allyn &Bacon.

National Maternal Child Resource Center on Cultural Competency. (1998). Cultural Diversity Curriculum Set for Social Workers and Health Practitioners. Austin, TX: University of Texas.

Novack, D.H, et al. (1997). Calibrating the Physician: Personal Awareness and Effective Patient Care. JAMA, 278(6), 502-509.

Robins, S.L., White, C.B., Alexander, G.L., Gruppen, L.D., & Grum, C.M. (2001). Assessing Medical Students ' Awareness of and Sensitivity to Diverse Health Beliefs Using a Standard Patient Station. Academic Medicine, 76(1), 46-80.

Ryan, M., & Twibell, R. (2002). Outcomes of a Transcultural Nursing Immersion Experience: Confirmation of a Dimensional Matrix. Journal of Transcultural Nursing, 13(1), 54-60.

References

Ryan, M., Hodson-Carlton, K., & Ali, N. (2000). Transcultural Nursing Concepts and Experiences in Nursing Curricula. Journal of Transcultural Nursing, 11(4), 300-307.

Ryan, M., Twibell, R., Bringham, C., & Bennett, P. (2000). Learning to Care for Clients in Their World, Not Mine. Journal of Nursing Education, 37(1), 3-4.

Smith, G., & Winfrey, M. (1998). Teaching Pathophysiology From a Multicultural Perspective. Nurse Educator, 23, 81-83.

St. Claire, A. (1999). Preparing Culturally Competent Practitioners. Journal of Nursing Education, 40(6), 270-275.

Suzuki, L.A., Ponterotto, J.G., & Meller, P.L. (2001). Handbook of Multicultural Assessment: Clinical, Psychological and Educational Applications. Jossey-Bass Publishers.

Var, R.M. (1998). Improving Educational Preparation For Transcultural Health Care. Nurse Educator Today, October Issue.

Weaver, H.N. (1998). Teaching Cultural Competence: Application of Experiential Learning Techniques. Journal of Teaching in Social Work, 17:65-79.

Welch, M. (1998). Required Curricula in Diversity and Cross-Cultural Medicine: The Time is now. Journal of the American Medical Women's Association, 53 (Suppl.), 121-123.

Welch, M. (1997). Enhancing Awareness of Diversity and Cultural Competence: A Workshop Series for Department Chairs and Course Directors. Acad. Med., 72:461-462.

Winn, J.M., & Riehl, G.K. (2001). Incorporating Transcultural Care Education in Allied Health Curricula. Journal of Allied Health, 30: 122-125.

Yoder, M. (2001). The Bridging Approach: Effective Strategies for Teaching Ethnically Diverse Nursing Students. Journal of Transcultural Nursing, 11(4), 319-325.

Zweifler, J., &Gonsalez, A.M. (1998). Teaching Residents to Care for Culturally Diverse Populations. Academic Medicine, 73(10), 1056-1061.

Annotated Website Links on Teaching Transcultural Health Care & Incorporating Cultural Concepts into the Health Professions' Curriculum

Cultural Competency Curriculum Modules Project

Sponsored by the American Institutes of Research and the U.S. Department of Health and Human Services Office of Minority Health. The project consists of the development and testing of a set of modules to train family physicians to be culturally competent according to the principles of the National Standards on Culturally and Linguistically Appropriate Services.

www.air.org/cccm

Diversity Web

A comprehensive compendium of campus practices and resources about diversity in higher education.

http://www.diversityweb.org/index.cfm

The Provision of Culturally Competent Health Care

This website is an article, by Blue (2000),that articulates the steps towards educating healthcare practitioners in the area of cultural competency.

http://www.musc.edu/deansclerkship/rccultur.html

STFM Core Curriculum Guidelines

Recommended core curriculum guidelines on culturally sensitive and competent health care.

http://www.stfm.org/corep.html

PRIME Diversity Project

Sponsored by the American Medical Students Association. The goal of the PRIME Project Cultural Competence Curriculum is to provide an adjunct model curriculum on cultural competence that will help physicians-in-training, as well as other health-related professions, to develop the attitudes, skills & knowledge base to effectively serve culturally and ethnically diverse populations, especially in underserved communities.

http://www.amsa.org/programs/prime.cfm

Website Links

Preparing Graduates to Meet the Needs of Diverse Populations

Conducted by the Southern Regional Education Board (SREB) Council on Collegiate Education for Nursing. This report examines how nursing education programs in the South are preparing graduates for these rapid changes in the ethnic composition of American society and includes findings from a 1997 survey.

http://www.sreb.org/programs/nursing/publications/diversepopulations.asp

Center for Healthy Families and Cultural Diversity

Department of Family Medicine/UMDNJ-Robert Wood Johnson Medical School and coordinated by Dr.Robert Like, this center was established in the1997-98 academic year, and is dedicated to leadership, advocacy, and excellence in promoting culturally-responsive, quality health care for diverse populations. It has evolved from a program focused primarily on multicultural education and training for health professionals, to an expanded and growing resource for technical assistance, consultation, and research/evaluation services.

http://www2.umdnj.edu/fmedweb/chfcd/INDEX.HTM

George Washington University Medical Center's Cultural Competence Module

Training modules on cultural competence.

http://www.gwu.edu/~iscopes/Cultcomp.htm

George Mason's Multicultural Early Childhood Team Training on Cultural Competence

Training modules on cultural competence.

http://apex.gmu.edu/mectt/module.html

Center for Cross-Cultural Health

Training units for educating healthcare providers in cultural competence.

http://www1.umn.edu/ccch/Training.htm--new.html

Website Links

National Multicultural Institute (NMI)
A collection of educational materials on diversity and cultural competency.
http://www.nmci.org

Multicultural Pavilion
Includes resources, such as experiential exercises on becoming
culturally competent, for educators and trainers.
http://curry.edschool.virginia.edu/go/multicultural/

Cultural Positivity
One component of this website is the "Perspectives of Differences "
curriculum. The program includes four Perspectives Of Differences
(PODs) for the individual trainee to learn the knowledge, skills and
attitudes needed to become a culturally competent healthcare provider.
http://www.gvhc.org/cultural/index.html

National Review of Nursing Education:Multicultural Nursing Education
This report, conducted by Maurice Eisenbruch, Professor of
Multicultural Health University of New South Wales, is a
comprehensive and international review of cultural competency in
nursing education.
http://www.dest.gov.au/highered/programmes/nursing reports.htm#research reports

Diversity Icebreakers: A Guide for Diversity Training
This website presents "icebreakers," which are short experiential activities
that can be used as openers in diversity training sessions to increase
awareness of diversity. The activities presented have been tested and
found effective in a wide variety of settings.
http://www.diversityresources.com/rc22/icebreak.html

Cultural Competency Curriculum Modules Project

This Web resource is developed based on the Cultural Competency
Handbook for Students, Faculty, and Staff compiled by R.Degano
and Dr. M. Disman for the Department of Public Health Sciences.
The Handbook has been compiled in response to frequent requests
from faculties, students and staff for resources on self-development
in knowledge and skills pertaining to diversity issues. This website
begins with an introduction section. Part two explores strategies for the
inclusion of diversity issues in curriculum. Part three contains selected
materials for personal reflection on cultural and racial diversity. Part
four comprises of various resources including books, journal articles,
journals, information sources, manuals, reports, audio-visual materials,
and services for students and faculties at the University of Toronto.
There is also a glossary section for key concepts and terminology.
http://www.phs.utoronto.ca/cultural_competency/mainmenu.htm

Toward Culturally Competent Care:A Toolbox for Teaching Communication Strategies

Developed by Mutha, Allen and Welch (Center for the Health Professions,
University of California, San Francisco), this 170-page curriculum is
organized into eleven sections that focus on teaching healthcare clinicians
to recognize cultural differences in patient interactions and use specific
communication skills to improve patient care. The materials can be adapted
for sequential one-hour sessions or for daylong seminars.
http://futurehealth.ucsf.edu/cnetwork/resources/curricula/diversity.html

JAMARDA Resources, Inc.

This website provides resources in cultural diversity training and
educational products for healthcare educators
http://www.jamardaresources.com/

Appendix C

"Ear-to-Ear Encounters: A Checklist for Culturally
Responsive Telephonic Communication"

(Campinha-Bacote, 2001)

Ear to Ear Encounters

ATTITUDES: Do you have any auditory stereotypes, prejudices or biases, based upon a person's speech pattern, dialect or tone of voice?

- What do you think when your client speaks with an "ethnic or cultural accent?"
- What are your thoughts when your client speaks "broken English?"
- What do you think about a person when he/she talks very fast or very slow?
- What are your beliefs about people with "southern accents?"
- What are your possible biases about people who have a "northern accent?"
- What are your initial thoughts when your client speaks very loud over the phone? Or very soft?
- Do you speak differently when you perceive that you are speaking with a female, as compared to a male? Why?
- After speaking with your client for one minute, do you have a mental picture of him/her? What is it and how does it influence your conversation with them?
- When you know you are speaking with a client, who is a professional (i.e., physician, nurse, teacher, lawyer, etc.), do you interact differently with them? How and why?

* REMEMBER: A person's speech pattern or dialect may not be related to their socioeconomic, educational, or intellectual level or their ability to understand what is being communicated. Speaking loudly may not represent anger; but rather a physical challenge such as deafness. Similarly, a soft-spoken voice may not represent shyness; but rather respect to the caller. We all have personal auditory biases based on our life experiences and must be careful not to allow these biases to interfere with effective telephonic communication.

KNOWLEDGE: What knowledge do you have about specific cultural/ethnic groups regarding what is considered culturally-sensitive telephonic communication?

- Do you assume that because a person has a last name like, Lopez, Rodriquez, Martinez, DaSilva, or Sanchez, that they are Hispanic/ Latino? If so, how is your conversation different?
- Are you knowledgeable that specific cultural groups may prefer one gender to speak with, as compared to another? How would you know this?
- Are you aware that although some clients may respond to you in English and say," Yes" or "No" they may have a limited proficiency of the English language and not truly understand what is being communicated?
- What is your response when you call a client and they do not speak English? Do you have knowledge of possible linguistic resources available to him/her?
- Are you knowledgeable of certain holidays that must be respected among specific ethnic/cultural groups, and avoid, if possible, to call on these days?

*REMEBER: The process of attaining culturally sensitive knowledge is intended to provide healthcare professionals with a general overview of different ethnic/cultural groups, not to stereotype cultural groups. There exists more variation within cultural/ethnic groups than across cultural/ethnic groups. Cultures are constantly evolving and no healthcare professional can hope to be completely familiar with all his/her clients' telephonic communication behaviors.

SKILLS: What skills do you have for effective telephonic encounters?

- How do you handle conflict over the telephone?
- How do you know if you offended your client?
- How do you assess the client's health beliefs, practices and customs in a sensitive way?
- How do you interpret silence?
- How do you assess if a client is physically challenged? (Are they blind? Can they read English? Can they read in their own language? Are they hearing impaired?)
- What constitutes "good" telephone behavior, for you?
- What constitutes "bad" or "rude" telephone behavior, for you?
- How do you convey caring over the telephone?
- How do you assess if a client is technologically challenged? (Do they have computer skills? What are their transportation resources?)

* **REMEMBER**: Obtaining cultural skill when communicating telephonically is a lifelong process. As Rolf Kerr stated, "Do not fear mistakes --- fear only the absence of creative, constructive and corrective responses to those mistakes." The goal is to generate a wide variety of culturally sensitive telephonic responses as well as to send and receive telephonic messages accurately and appropriately in each culturally different context (adapted from Sue, et. al, 1982). Healthcare professionals must remember that what constitutes "good" or "bad" telephone behavior for them, may not be the same for specific cultural/ethnic groups. For example, if a client interrupts you frequently during a telephone conversation, it may demonstrate a sign of enthusiasm and interest, and not a rude telephone behavior. The key to successful telephonic communication is to reflect a caring attitude. "People don't care how much you know, until they first know how much you care."

Appendix D

Inventory for Assessing the Process of Cultural
Competence Among Healthcare Professionals - Revised
(IAPCC-R)

(Campinha-Bacote, 2002)

Inventory for Assessing The Process of Cultural Competence Among Healthcare Professionals - Revised (IAPCC-R)

(Copyrighted 2002, Campinha-Bacote)

1. **Cultural competence mainly refers to one's competency concerning different ethnic groups.**
   STRONGLY AGREE   AGREE   DISAGREE   STRONGLY DISAGREE

2. **I feel that cultural competence is an ongoing process.**
   STRONGLY AGREE   AGREE   DISAGREE   STRONGLY DISAGREE

3. **Factors such as geographical location, gender, religious affiliation, sexual orientation, and occupation are not considered areas of concern when seeking cultural competence.**
   STRONGLY AGREE   AGREE   DISAGREE   STRONGLY DISAGREE

4. **I have a personal commitment to care for clients from ethnically/culturally diverse groups.**
   STRONGLY AGREE   AGREE   DISAGREE   STRONGLY DISAGREE

5. **I feel that there is a relationship between culture and health.**
   STRONGLY AGREE   AGREE   DISAGREE   STRONGLY DISAGREE

6. **I am knowledgeable in the area of ethnic pharmacology.**
   VERY KNOWLEDGEABLE   KNOWLEDGEABLE   SOMEWHAT KNOWLEDGEABLE   NOT KNOWLEDGEABLE

7. **I am motivated to care for clients from culturally/ethnically diverse groups.**
   STRONGLY AGREE   AGREE   DISAGREE   STRONGLY DISAGREE

8. **I am knowledgeable about the worldviews, beliefs, practices and/or life ways of at least two cultural groups.**
   VERY KNOWLEDGEABLE   KNOWLEDGEABLE   SOMEWHAT KNOWLEDGEABLE   NOT KNOWLEDGEABLE

9. **I am aware of the cultural limitations of existing assessment tools that are used with ethnic groups.**
   VERY AWARE   AWARE   SOMEWHAT AWARE   NOT AWARE

10. **I am knowledgeable in the area of biological variations among different ethnic groups.**
    VERY KNOWLEDGEABLE   KNOWLEDGEABLE   SOMEWHAT KNOWLEDGEABLE   NOT KNOWLEDGEABLE

11. **Anatomical and physiological variations do not exist in different ethnic groups.**
    STRONGLY AGREE   AGREE   DISAGREE   STRONGLY DISAGREE

12. **I am aware of specific diseases common among different ethnic groups .**
    VERY AWARE   AWARE   SOMEWHAT AWARE   NOT AWARE

13. **I am willing to learn from others as cultural informants.**
    STRONGLY AGREE   AGREE   DISAGREE   STRONGLY DISAGREE

14. **I seek out education, consultation, and/or training experiences to enhance my understanding and effectiveness with culturally and ethnically diverse clients.**
    STRONGLY AGREE   AGREE   DISAGREE   STRONGLY DISAGREE

IAPCC-R

15. **I am aware of at least 2 institutional barriers that prevent cultural/ethnic groups from seeking healthcare services.**

    VERY AWARE   AWARE   SOMEWHAT AWARE   NOT AWARE

16. **I recognize the limits of my competence when interacting with culturally/ethnically diverse clients.**

    STRONGLY AGREE   AGREE   DISAGREE   STRONGLY DISAGREE

17. **When my values and beliefs "clash" with my client's values and beliefs I become frustrated.**

    STRONGLY AGREE   AGREE   DISAGREE   STRONGLY DISAGREE

18. **I am aware of some of the stereotyping attitudes, preconceived notions and feelings that I have toward members of other ethnic/cultural groups.**

    VERY AWARE   AWARE   SOMEWHAT AWARE   NOT AWARE

19. **I have a passion for caring for clients from culturally/ethnically diverse groups.**

    STRONGLY AGREE   AGREE   DISAGREE   STRONGLY DISAGREE

20. **I am aware of at least 2 cultural assessment tools to be used when assessing clients in a healthcare setting.**

    VERY AWARE   AWARE   SOMEWHAT AWARE   NOT AWARE

21. **It is more important to conduct a cultural assessment on ethnically diverse clients than with other clients.**

    STRONGLY AGREE   AGREE   DISAGREE   STRONGLY DISAGREE

22. **I feel comfortable in asking questions that relate to the client's ethnic/cultural background.**

    VERY COMFORTABLE   COMFORTABLE   SOMEWHAT COMFORTABLE   NOT COMFORTABLE

23. **I am involved with cultural/ethnic groups outside of my healthcare setting role.**

    VERY INVOLVED   INVOLVED   SOMEWHAT INVOLVED   NOT INVOLVED

24. **I believe that one must "want to" become culturally competent if cultural competence is to be achieved.**

    STRONGLY AGREE   AGREE   DISAGREE   STRONGLY DISAGREE

25. **I believe that there are more differences within cultural groups than across cultural groups.**

    STRONGLY AGREE   AGREE   DISAGREE   STRONGLY DISAGREE

Application:

The IAPCC-R is designed to measure the level of cultural competence among healthcare professionals in all healthcare settings.

Informants:

The IAPCC-R is specifically intended for the following healthcare professionals: physicians, physician assistants, medical students, licensed practical or vocational nurses, registered nurses, advanced practice nurses, nursing students, medical and nursing faculty, and clinical pharmacists. With modifications, the IAPCC-R can be used with other healthcare professionals and allied health professions.

Development of the Instrument:

The IAPCC-R is a revision of the Inventory for Assessing the Process of Cultural Competence Among Healthcare Professionals (IAPCC). The IAPCC was developed by Campinha-Bacote in 1997 and is based on her model of cultural competence, *The Process of Cultural Competence in the Delivery of Healthcare Services*, 1998, 3rd Edition. However, the IAPCC only measured four of the five constructs of this model (cultural awareness, cultural knowledge, cultural skill and cultural encounters; not the fifth construct of cultural desire). In 2003, Campinha-Bacote developed the IAPCC-R, in which she added five additional questions to the IAPCC to measure the fifth construct of cultural desire.

Administration:

The IAPCC-R is a self-administered tool. It consists of 25 items that measure the five cultural constructs of desire, awareness, knowledge, skill and encounters. There are 5 items that address each one of these constructs. The IAPCC-R uses a 4-point likert scale reflecting the response categories of strongly agree, agree, disagree, strongly disagree; very aware, aware, somewhat aware, not aware; very knowledgeable, knowledgeable, somewhat knowledgeable, not knowledgeable; very comfortable, comfortable, somewhat comfortable, not comfortable; and very involved, involved, somewhat involved, not involved. Completion time is approximately 10-15 minutes. Scores indicate whether a healthcare professional is operating at a level of cultural proficiency, cultural competence, cultural awareness or cultural incompetence. Higher scores depict a higher level of competence.

Reliability and Validity of the Instrument:

Koempel (2003) conducted a study with 275 nurse practitioners using the IAPCC-R and calculated the following reliability scores: Reliability Coefficient Cronbach alpha = .85; Guttman Split-half = .83. Spencer and Cooper-Brathwaite (2003) conducted a study of 50 public health nurses working in Toronto, Canada. Their data analysis revealed: Reliability Coefficient Cronbach Alpha = .90. Content validity of the IAPCC-R was established by national experts in the field of transcultural health care. Construct validity was addressed by linking the IAPCC-R with Campinha-Bacote's (1998) conceptual model of cultural competence.

Duplication/Copying of Instrument:

The IAPCC-R is copyrighted and formal permission to use the tool is required. It is only available through purchasing the book , "The Process of Cultural Competence in the Delivery of Healthcare Services," 4th Edition (2003), authored by Campinha-Bacote (please refer to the website, www.transculturalcare.net, for an order form to obtain this book). To obtain permission to use the IAPCC-R, please send your request (include how you plan to use the tool) along with a self-addressed and stamped envelop to:

Dr. Josepha Campinha-Bacote
11108 Huntwicke Place
Cincinnati, OH 45241

IAPCC-R Scoring Key

ITEMS # 2, 4, 5, 7, 13, 14, 16, 19, 24, 25

4 pts. = Strongly Agree

3 pts. = Agree

2 pts. = Disagree

1 pt. = Strongly Disagree

ITEMS # 1, 3, 11, 17, 21

4 pts. = Strongly Disagree

3 pts. = Disagree

2 pts. = Agree

1 pt. = Strongly Agree

ITEMS # 6, 8, 10

4 pts. = Very Knowledgeable

3 pts. = Knowledgeable

2 pts. = Somewhat Knowledgeable

1 pt. = Not Knowledgeable

ITEMS # 9, 12, 15, 18, 20

4 pts. = Very Aware

3 pts. = Aware

2 pts. = Somewhat Aware

1 pt. = Not Aware

ITEM # 23

4 pts. = Very Involved

3 pts. = Involved

2 pts. = Somewhat Involved

1 pt. = Not Involved

ITEM #22

4 pts. = Very Comfortable

3 pts. = Comfortable

2 pts. = Somewhat Comfortable

1 pt. = Not Comfortable

The extent to which a healthcare professional is culturally competent is indicated by the following category ranges:

Culturally Proficient	91 -100
Culturally Competent	75 -90
Culturally Aware	51 -74
Culturally Incompetent	25 -50

Josepha Campinha-Bacote

"The real leader serves truth, not people..."

J. B. Yeats

Josepha Campinha-Bacote is the President and Founder of Transcultural C.A.R.E. Associates, a private consultation service which focuses on clinical, administrative, research, and educational issues in transcultural health care and mental health. She has worked with medical centers, healthcare organizations, academic institutions, community outreach centers, managed care organizations and the federal government to enhance the level of cultural competence among their healthcare professionals.

She received her B.S. degree from the University of Rhode Island, her M.S. degree from Texas Women's University, and her Ph.D degree from the University of Virginia. She is currently pursuing a graduate degree in Theological Studies. She is Board Certified by the American Nurses Credentialing Center as an Adult Clinical Nurse Specialist in Psychiatric & Mental Health Nursing, certified by the Transcultural Nursing Society as a Certified Transcultural Nurse, and holds a Certificate of Authority by the Ohio Board of Nursing to practice as an Advanced Practice Clinical Nurse Specialist. In addition, Dr. Campinha-Bacote holds the academic title of Adjunct Faculty at several universities including The Ohio State University in Columbus, Ohio and the University of Cincinnati, in Cincinnati Ohio.

She has been the recipient of several national and international honors and awards, including the Distinguished Lecturer Award from Sigma Theta Tau International, the Post-Doctoral Research Fellowship Award from the Ohio Department of Mental Health, and the Ethnic/Racial Minority Fellowship Award from the National Institute of Mental Health. She is also a Fellow of the American Academy of Nursing.

Dr. Campinha-Bacote has given more than 1,000 national and international presentations on issues concerning transcultural health care and transcultural psychiatry and has published over 50 articles in these specialty areas. Several colleges of nursing, pharmacy, social work, medicine and other allied healthcare disciplines are incorporating her model, *The Process of Cultural Competence in The Delivery of Healthcare Services,* into their undergraduate and graduate programs.

In 2000, Dr. Campinha-Bacote served on the National Advisory Committee to the U.S. Department of Health and Human Services Office of Minority Health to develop standards for Culturally and Linguistically Appropriate Services (CLAS) in Health Care. She currently serves as a consultant to the National Center For Cultural Competence (NCCC) in Washington, DC and to the Health Resources and Services Administration (HRSA) Managed Care Technical Assistance Center of the U.S. Department of Health and Human Services.

Dr. Campinha-Bacote can be contacted by sending an e-mail to meddir@aol.com, or visiting her website at www.transculturalcare.net